Seeking the Right Path

About the Author

JOHN MUCAI HOLDS A PH.D. in Business Administration from the University of Nairobi. He is also a Certified Public Accountant of Kenya. He is an alumnus of United States International University, where he graduated with an MSc in Management and Organizational Development and cum laude in BSc in Information Systems & Technology. He retired from Coca-Cola East & Central Africa Ltd in 2017 and has since been pursuing various hobbies and entrepreneurial interests.

Seeking the Right Path

A search for spiritual enlightenment

John Mucai

For any further information, contact John Muigai Mucai at the following address:
P.O. Box 2069 - 00606, Nairobi, Kenya. Email:
johnmucai@gmail.com

Cover design by Linda Matama

ISBN 978-9966-955-09-8

Contents

Foreword

"SEEKING THE RIGHT PATH" is the fifth in the MUCAI Quick Read series of books. The books in the series are for the reader who has a few hours on their hands that they could use to indulge in light and educative entertainment. For example, a passenger on a bus, train, cruise ship, or plane heading to a distant destination, a tourist relaxing on a beach on the beautiful coast of Mombasa, or someone just relaxing at home after a long day at work.

The books in the series cover a broad spectrum of topics to titillate the reader's intellect:

- humorous biographical stories
- accounts of captivating historical events
- narratives of extraordinary science
- journeys towards spiritual enlightenment
- intrigues in business
- strategy, and
- thought-provoking philosophical ideas

The series encourages the reader to think about the world differently and positively. Please visit *mucaiquickread.com* for more information on the series.

John Mucai

Preface

I AM ONE OF OVER two billion people who profess the Christian faith. However, I have often wondered why Christianity is not accessible to several more billions of people and if this limitation was part of God's plan. And if not, why would God let such a situation persist? I do not doubt that followers of other faiths ask similar questions but from different viewpoints.

The quest to seek answers to these questions must start with an understanding and appreciation of the multiple religions in this world. Gaining such an understanding would most likely reveal that the fundamental beliefs of all faiths are rooted in the everlasting human search for the meaning of life—a search rooted in the mystery of birth and ultimate death.

Further, there is a common desire for spiritual awakening and salvation. The differences between religions are merely different ways of fulfilling this desire. If this is the case, gaining even a superficial understanding of the religious beliefs of "others" would reveal more commonalities than differences.

This enlightenment would be the foundation of a more cohesive world community based on mutual respect. In this book, I attempt to seek such an understanding, using the lenses of a layman but with a slight philosophical twist to provide a structure to the inquiry.

I have divided the book into five parts. The first part is an introduction. I set the book's high-level context and inspiration. I outline the different belief systems, emphasizing Christianity, Islam, Hinduism, and Buddhism. The focus on these four religions is because they have the most substantial following globally. Their followers account for approximately 80% of the world's population.[1]

In the second part, I explore the relationship between religion and culture and religion and science. I have included examples of schisms between religious and cultural practices in recent history.

I have devoted the book's third part to critical philosophical questions about religion, focusing primarily on the four major religions and their sacred texts. I have reviewed the holy texts critically to elicit the most significant insights. The underlying rationale is that the texts have been the subject of inquiry for centuries. Therefore, the wisdom they contain should be easily accessible through research on the internet. Also, seeking the truth, no matter how bitter the finding, must be the right thing to do for the utmost spiritual enlightenment. I have also attempted to find answers from philosophical and other perspectives.

In the fourth part of the book, I have given my perspectives on the big questions that emerge from Chapter Three based on the insights from the review presented in the preceding chapters.

The fifth and final part of the book is a practical personal example of living in faith. Any reader who wishes to share their experience based on another religious faith is welcome to offer their input. I will gladly include it in the next edition of this book, within practical limits, depending upon the number and length of suggestions I receive.

I hope every reader finds something valuable in this book that will give their life a better meaning.

Acknowledgments

The Almighty God has been the shining guiding light throughout my life, even in this book project. I will always remain steadfastly thankful to Him.

This book project would not have been possible without the support of my wife, Susan, my son Allan, and my daughter Anne. All of them provided invaluable assistance in reviewing the book. I owe them a significant debt of gratitude.

I would also like to thank Teddy Muhia and Nzisa Kattambo for their invaluable contributions in editing the book.

Part One

A Quest for Understanding

Chapter 1

Introduction

*"I do not feel obliged to believe that the
same God who has endowed us with
sense, reason, and intellect has intended
us to forgo their use."*
-Galileo Galilei

SOMETIME IN 1996, I WENT on a short visit to Ongata Rongai, a small town about 20 kilometers from Nairobi, on the way to Lake Magadi. I finished my engagement at around 4:00 pm. On my way home, I stopped at a small shopping center about five kilometers from the Bomas of Kenya. I spent about five minutes there. I then headed back to my car. I did not realize that there was someone following me. And just after I opened the car door, the person following me vigorously pushed me into the car and occupied the driver's seat. Another person suddenly appeared from nowhere and occupied the front passenger seat.

Before I could utter even a word, the person in the passenger seat grabbed me by the neck and pulled my head to his knees in a firm stranglehold.

The person who had occupied the driver's seat took control of the car and drove away. I had no idea where we were heading. I could hardly breathe, considering the very tight stranglehold on my neck.

After about ten minutes, the car turned onto a rough road. At this point, I realized I was in terrible danger, but there was nothing I could do.

I was the victim of a violent hijack.

Twenty or so minutes later, the car stopped. It was in the middle of a thick forest with no sight of human habitation. The two people forced me out of the vehicle. There was a bit of a struggle. They overpowered me and pushed me into the boot of the car. Then they drove off. By that time, I had been injured and completely disoriented.

I did not know where the car was heading or what would eventually happen to me.

I was to remain in the darkness of the car boot for several hours.

From time to time, during that dreadful night, all I could hear in my dazed condition were the unintelligible conversations of the two thugs and intermittent activity inside and outside the vehicle:

The car would stop.
A passenger would enter the car.
The car would drive off.
A few minutes later, the car would stop again.
The thugs would forcibly remove the passenger.
Some commotion would occur outside the vehicle.
The thugs would return to the vehicle.
The car would drive off again.
After a few more minutes, the car would stop again.
A new passenger would enter the vehicle.
Thugs would treat the new passenger as the first one.

After some time, I figured the two hijackers were probably picking up people waiting for public transport. They would probably drive to a deserted location and rob them.

This routine continued for several hours, except for a brief moment when everything went silent. I had lost my sense of time. After this short interlude, the thugs returned to the car and drove off again.

At around 2:00 am (as I learned later), the thugs got involved in an accident with a taxi on Uhuru Highway, near the University of Nairobi roundabout. After a brief exchange with the taxi driver, the two thugs, who I later learned were drunk, pretended they had gone to look for the police. They then disappeared into the city center.

After some time, the taxi driver called the police. When the police arrived, they inspected the cars and recorded the necessary details. They then arranged for a truck to tow my vehicle to the Traffic Police Headquarters near Kenyatta National Hospital along Ngong Road.

All that time, I was in the car boot. I had no idea what was happening. I was completely disoriented, mainly because of injuries I had sustained while being forced into the car boot. At one stage, I heard the sound of chains. Later, I learned that the sound was from the chain winch of the towing truck as the police and the towing truck driver hoisted my car onto the truck for towing to the Traffic Police Headquarters.

After about 30 minutes, I heard the sound of the chains once again. The sound lasted for a short time. It then became bizarrely silent, an eerie silence that I could not understand.

I assumed the hijackers had arrived at their destination and had decided to go to sleep or abandon the car. Whatever it was, there was nothing that I could do. I just waited!

◆◆◆

It began freezing briefly later, indicating that morning was setting in. It was still dark in the boot, but strangely, I could sense it was no longer dark outside.

At some point, I heard people passing by talking in low tones. By this time, I was feeling less disoriented. I decided to take a chance and started knocking on the roof of the boot. The passersby seemed to have been perplexed by the knocking sound. They stopped and started inquiring who was in the boot.

They tried to open the car but without much luck. The hijackers had locked the vehicle and taken the keys. I suggested that the passersby break one of the windows and pull the door latch to open the doors. After gaining entry, they opened the boot using the boot opening lever.

◆◆◆

An immense feeling of relief engulfed me when I emerged from the boot and saw that the people who had opened the boot were policemen.

They were policemen from the Traffic Police Headquarters. One of them went into the office immediately and brought me his tracksuit to wear over my disheveled clothes.

I explained what had happened to the police officers. I could sense their incredible feelings of pity and anger. They invited me to the police station, where I telephoned my wife, Susan, to inform her of my whereabouts. I also recorded a brief official statement.

Fortunately, the police station was close to Nairobi Hospital. And after a few minutes, the police officers took me there for treatment.

◆◆◆

Several things flash through my mind whenever I reflect on this horrifying incident.

Firstly, the accident at the University roundabout was not serious, but the event miraculously halted the hijackers' progress. I wonder what could have happened if that accident did not occur. Where would the hijackers have taken me? What would they have done to me after their nocturnal criminal spree?

Secondly, when the towing truck took my car to the Traffic Police Headquarters at Ngong Road, they parked it a few meters from some offices, near a path used by the police officers when they walked to the office every morning.

If the truck driver had decided to park the car a few meters further, in the section where other vehicles involved in accidents were typically parked, the probability of my rescue by the police officers would have been minimal.

Thirdly, the Traffic Police Headquarters was near a major hospital. So, I received excellent medical attention very quickly after my rescue.

Fourthly, when the doctors at the hospital examined me, it turned out that I had not sustained severe internal injuries.

◆◆◆

When I eventually left the hospital, I experienced something else that I will never forget: immense love and consideration from my wife and children, my parents, brothers, sisters, relatives, neighbors, workmates, and my employer. I could see the outrage written on each of their faces as they tried to digest the horror the thugs visited upon me on that unfortunate night. Their words of sympathy and consolation made a tremendous difference and enabled my speedy recovery.

However, one incident of extreme insensitivity from unexpected quarters astounded me. But I forgave the person involved and was able to have internal peace and move on with life.

◆◆◆

That unfortunate hijacking incident taught me two big lessons. First, I learned that every moment is the most precious thing we can ever have. Second, there must be a deep meaning in life worth seeking, a meaning that one can only find through spiritual enlightenment.

◆◆◆

It is not easy to imagine how life would be without religion. The world is so complex and difficult to understand that without religion to give one a bearing, life's journey would be without much hope.

But then the question arises: what is religion, and what religion should one follow? Is there one clear path one can confidently follow without any doubt about beliefs that concrete reality cannot support? This question is complex, and undoubtedly, theologians study it in detail in theological institutions.

However, not everybody can afford to study theology under the tutelage of professional theologians and scholars. But that should not be a handicap in the quest for spiritual enlightenment. Today, there are numerous freely accessible sources where one can search for any type of knowledge, including religion. This book attempts to seek wisdom from these sources.

I do not intend to make this a book on theology or promote a particular doctrine. The book is about an ordinary world citizen's journey to seek spiritual enlightenment by sifting through the literature on different religious faiths, particularly Christianity, Islam, Hinduism, and Buddhism. These religions have a combined following of about 80% of the world's population. Hopefully, the reader will find value in joining me on my journey.

Chapter 2

What is Religion?

"To know that we know what we know,
and to know that we do not know what
we do not know, that is true knowledge."
-Nicolaus Copernicus

BEFORE WE MOVE TOO FAR in our journey, we must ask ourselves one key question: What is religion? There may be as many answers to this question as theologians and philosophers. We need to align on the definition of religion to prevent flaws in our conclusions when we reach our destination.

As Mbiti (2006) states, a misunderstanding of what constitutes religion resulted in the denigration of African religious practices by the Western countries that colonized African countries.

There are records of many atrocities committed against the African people in an attempt to eradicate what the Westerners perceived as primitive animist practices that were anathema to Western religions. The Western missionaries dismissed African religious rituals as paganism and superstition. Other deprecating adjectives that they used were "crude," "fetish," and "uncivilized."[2,3]

Mbiti elucidates the idea of religion in an African context, notably that religion is part of the African person's life. Indeed, before the advent of the colonizers from Western countries, almost every one of the more than 1,000 African tribes had its own religion and religious practices. The same can be said of people in other parts of the world, as we shall see when we look at the mainstream religions around the globe.[4]

So, how should we define religion? Frederick Ferre offers a holistic definition encompassing all world religions, including those that do not believe in a deity:

Religion is the most intensive and comprehensive method of valuing that is experienced by humankind.[5]

In our case, we will adopt the more straightforward definition in the Oxford Desk Dictionary, namely, that religion is:

n. 1 belief in a personal God or gods entitled to obedience and worship 2 expression of this in worship 3 particular system of faith and worship 4 thing that one is devoted to.[6]

Accordingly, we will ignore the practices that some people may associate with certain religions, such as black magic and witchcraft, practiced in different parts of the world.

Chapter 3

Different Types of Religions

"God has no religion."
—Mahatma Gandhi.

ABOUT 84% OF THE WORLD'S PEOPLE identify themselves with one religion or another, and this ratio is rising.[7,8] According to the Pew Research Center (2019), Christians comprise the largest religious group, with a membership of 2.38 billion, followed by Islam, which has 1.91 billion followers. Hinduism is third, with a following of 1.16 billion, while Buddhism is fourth, with 507 million followers. There are many other religious groups.[9,10]

However, the interesting statistic is that about 1.2 billion people today, comprising 16% of the world's population, are not adherents of any particular religious group. These are not necessarily atheists but people who do not associate with any specific religious group.

If these 1.2 billion people were to form a religion, it would be the third-largest religion after Christianity and Islam.[11,12]

Other notable religious groups with a significant number of members include Sikhism with 23 million; Yoruba with 20 million; Juche with 19 million; Judaism with 14 million; Baha'i with 6 million; Jainism with 4 million; Shinto with 4 million; Cao Dai with 3 million; and Tenrikyo with 2.4 million followers.[13]

A notable feature of many religions is that they are divided into smaller groupings. For example, Christianity is divided into Catholics and multiple other protestant denominations. Islam is divided into Sunni, Shia, Ibadi, Ahmadiyya, and Sufi. Hinduism is divided into Vaishnavism, Shaivism, Shaktism, and Smartism. On the other hand, Buddhism has two main groupings, Theravāda and Mahayana. In the case of Jews, the sub-division is between Orthodox, Conservative, Reform, and other smaller groups.[14]

Another interesting feature of religions is that they all seem concentrated in particular regions. For example, followers of Hinduism and Buddhism are concentrated in the Asia-Pacific region. In contrast, followers of Islam are mainly found in the Middle East. Christianity, on the other hand, is concentrated in 157 different countries.[15]

Another fascinating statistic is that Islam is growing faster than any other religion and is projected to overtake Christianity by around 2050 in terms of total membership.

The relatively fast growth of Islam compared to Christianity is mainly attributable to the relatively higher population growth rates of Muslims than Christians. Muslim mothers tend to have more children than Christian mothers. A gradual decline in Christianity in Western Europe is also a contributory factor.[16]

Interestingly, only two countries have special seats in parliament reserved for religious leaders: Iran and the United Kingdom.[17]

Islam is the state religion in 27 countries. Christianity is the state religion in 13 countries, including the Vatican, where the Pope is the head of state.[18]

There are other interesting facts about religion. For example, there is an internet religion called *Kopimism* that has been in existence since 2010 in Sweden. Followers of the religion believe that information is holy and that the act of copying computer files is sacred.[19,20]

The Missionary Church of Kopism, founded by Isak Gerson and Gustav Nipe, is not just a belief system but an officially recognized religion by the government of Sweden. Their sacrament, known as "kopyacting," Involves believers copying information in communion with each other online, primarily through sharing files.[21]

Other unusual religions exist, such as the Church of the Flying Spaghetti Monster (*Pastafarianism*), which the government of New Zealand recognizes.[22]

Chapter 4

Religious Teachings

"Human beings must be known to be loved, but Divine beings must be loved to be known."
-Blaise Pascal

WITH THE HUGE PLETHORA OF religions today, how can one know the true religion? Or, more importantly, is there a way of determining the most suitable faith to follow? The answer may be to follow the religion one was introduced to by their parents. But is that all? Should one not attempt to discover what is taught in different faiths and decide independently? Or could all of the world's religions be just different shades of one fundamental belief system? In that event, it would not matter what religion one pursued. Hopefully, by the end of this Chapter, we will have gained insights that will help us answer these questions.

Introduction to Religious Faiths

Given the many religions in the world, it would be difficult to explore them all. We will examine only the four major ones: Christianity, Islam, Hinduism, and Buddhism.

The idea is not to explore the deep aspects of a particular religion. It would be dishonest to suggest that we can delve into such details in a book of this nature. Some aspects of religion can only be fully appreciated through total immersion, and such immersion would be impractical for our purposes, given our limited scope.

However, we are fortunate to live in an age when many religious beliefs and practices have been codified in documents. Many such records are easily accessible electronically via the Internet or in libraries.

This book articulates the different belief systems on the premise that truth is a core virtue of all religions. Therefore, the information is presented as objectively as possible to gain the most profound insight.

The information in this book should be familiar to every believer of the faith in question. In some instances, the information presented may seem unpalatable to a follower of a particular religion. However, true knowledge must surely come from confronting the facts, no matter what they are. That perspective notwithstanding, utmost consideration is given to the feelings of the followers of each religion.

CHRISTIANITY

The number of books written on Christianity is mind-boggling. However, the fundamental Christian teachings are contained in the Holy Bible. So, by reading the Bible, we ought to clearly understand the Christian faith. But how did the Bible come into being?

The Holy Bible

The Bible is the most influential book ever published. More than 5 billion copies have been sold to date, excluding the 100 million copies given out free of charge annually. It is a sacred text for Christians—sales of the Bible average 100 million copies annually.[23]

In 397 A.D., the Catholic Council of Carthage selected the 66 books of the Bible from multiple sources.[24]

The Bible is comprised of the Old and New Testaments. The Old Testament chronicles the relationship between the Jewish people and their God, Yahweh. On the other hand, the New Testament chronicles Jesus Christ's life history and teachings.

There are 39 books in the Old Testament and 27 in the New Testament. Notably, the Bible used by Catholics contains 14 additional books of the New Testament, known as the Apocrypha.[25]

The original manuscripts of the Bible do not exist, but this fact may be irrelevant to Christians who firmly believe that the words in the Bible are divinely inspired.[26]

The Old Testament was originally written in Hebrew and Aramaic in some sections. In contrast, the original manuscripts of the New Testament were written in Greek. The Bible was subsequently translated into multiple languages.

The Bible was written by various people, starting around 1000 BC, based on oral literature handed down from generation to generation. However, it is not 100% clear who wrote the different chapters. Yet, historians and theologians have, over the years, made reasonable guesses on who the authors were.[27]

The Bible has been edited several times over the ages. The three main editions are the King James Bible, the Gutenberg Bible, and the Dead Sea Scrolls.[28]

In 1611, King James I of England and Ireland mandated a translation of the Bible. The King James version was intended to supersede all previously printed English Bibles, including the Great Bible translation mandated by Henry VIII in 1539 and the Bishops' Bible produced in 1568 during the rule of Elizabeth I.[29]

The Gutenberg Bible was printed in 1454 using Johannes Gutenberg's new printing technology. Johann Furst and Peter Schöffer financed the printing, facilitating cheap and large-quantity printing.

This development was significant because it made the Bible freely accessible to many members of the public who could read English.[30]

◆◆◆

The Dead Sea Scrolls are 800-page fragments of the Old Testament (excluding the Book of Esther) discovered by a Bedouin shepherd in November 1946 and February 1947 in a cave at Wadi Qumran in the Dead Sea area. Scientific measurements indicated that the scrolls were written between 200 BC and the 1st Century AD.

The scrolls' discovery was an immensely significant archaeological finding, mesmerizing many archaeologists and theologians. Many fragments of the scrolls are currently preserved at the Shrine of the Book, part of the Israel Museum in Jerusalem.[31]

◆◆◆

The Jews divided the Old Testament into three sections. The first section is the *Torah*, covering the first five books. The second section is the *Nabiim, which consists* of texts believed to have been written by several prophets, including Ezekiel, Jeremiah, and Malachi. The third section, *Khetaim*, contains poetic books, including Psalms, Proverbs, Ecclesiastes, and Job.[32]

On the other hand, the New Testament is divided into four sets of books. These are the gospels of Mathew, Mark, Luke, and John. Theologians believe that Mathew and St. Paul wrote these books. Secondly, the book of Acts is a historical account of the life of Jesus Christ. The third set comprises the 13 epistles books, comprising the letters that Jesus's disciple Paul wrote to various congregations. The fourth is Revelations, which John wrote. It is referred to as "apocalyptic" as it narrates the apocalypse that will occur at the end of time when God will come back to earth and judge the living and the dead.[33]

Core Beliefs of Christians

One of the fundamental beliefs of Christianity is that there is only one God. God manifests himself in three forms: God the Father, Son, and the Holy Spirit. Jesus Christ is regarded as God the Son. This triad of manifestations is referred to as the holy trinity.

Christians believe that God created the earth and the heavens. God is also all-powerful, present everywhere, knows everything, and loves everyone on earth. Further, people can have a personal relationship with God through prayer and continual worship.[34]

Another fundamental belief of Christianity is that there is life after death. And that those who repent their sins and follow the teachings of Jesus Christ will ultimately go to Heaven, while those who do not repent will end up in hell.[35]

Christians believe that they can communicate with God through prayer. Prayers, in different forms, are central to the rituals of Christian churches.[36]

Christians believe that Jesus is God who came to earth and lived like an ordinary human being. Further, Jesus was born by the virgin Mary, conceived of the Holy Spirit.[37]

Additionally, Christians believe that Jesus was subjected to suffering and crucified on the cross, died, and then resurrected. And that his death allowed those who believed in him to repent and have their sins forgiven.[38]

The Church is where Christians congregate in prayer and come together to celebrate the holy sacrament. The sacrament is a re-enactment of the Last Supper (the Eucharist), the final meal Jesus shared with his disciples before the Romans crucified him.[39]

Every Christian undergoes a ritual of baptism as a sign of their belief in the teachings of Jesus Christ. It is customary in some Christian churches to take a new name upon baptism as a sign that one has become a new person.[40]

Over time, many different Christian denominations have emerged with minor differences in beliefs and rituals.[41] For example, the Presbyterian Church of East Africa's core beliefs are encapsulated in the Apostles Creed, which reads as follows:

I believe in God, the Father almighty,
Creator of heaven and earth,
and in Jesus Christ,
his only Son, our Lord,

who was conceived
by the Holy Spirit,
born of the Virgin Mary,
suffered under Pontius Pilate,
was crucified, died, and was buried;
he descended into hell;
on the third day, he rose again from the dead;
he ascended into heaven
and is seated at the right hand
Of the Father almighty;
from there, he will come
To judge the living and the dead.
I believe in the Holy Spirit,
the holy catholic Church,
the communion of saints,
the forgiveness of sins,
the resurrection of the body,
and life everlasting. Amen.[42,43]

It should be noted that what is presented above is but a snapshot of Christianity. There is much more about Christianity, some of which we will cover in subsequent chapters.

ISLAM

The literature on Islam is enormous, but the fundamental beliefs are the same. Muslims believe that Muhammad was a prophet who was anointed to spread the word of God to humanity. The Quran, the Hadith, and the Sunnah contain the basic tenets of Islam.

A Muslim convert is required to perform five primary duties. Firstly, to profess the faith (*shahada*). One way of doing this is by uttering as often as possible the words: "I bear witness that there is no god but Allah and that Muhammad is his prophet."

Secondly, a Muslim must pray (*salat*) five times daily: at dawn, noon, mid-afternoon, sunset, and evening. These prayers are called *subh*, *zuhr*, *asr*, *maghrib*, and *isha*.

Thirdly, Muslims must express their devotion to God through almsgiving (*zakat*). The *zakat* is obligatory. Voluntary giving to charity is called *sadaqa*.

The fourth duty of a Muslim is fasting (*sawm*) during Ramadan. Traditionally, fasting begins at the first sighting of the moon and continues from daybreak to sunset for one month. During fasting, a Muslim is not allowed to eat, drink, or engage in sexual relations. There are exceptions, for example, for travelers and the sick. The fast-breaking at the end of the month is called *Eid al Fitr*.

The fifth duty is to go on at least one pilgrimage (*hajj*) to Mecca. Several rituals are performed in Mecca, culminating with the *Eid Al Adha* festival at the end of the pilgrimage.[44]

The Holy Quran

The Quran is the sacred scripture of Islam. It contains the teachings of Prophet Muhammad. Followers of Islam believe that the words in the Quran are the words of God that were dictated to Muhammad by God's angel, Gabriel.[45]

To fully appreciate the Quran, it is crucial to understand the life of Muhammad.

◆◆◆

Muhammad was born in 570 CE in Mecca, a trading and religious Centre. He was born into a family of humble means belonging to the Quraysh tribe. His father, Abdullah, died before Muhammad was born. When Muhammad reached the age of six, his mother, Aminah, died, too. Muhammad was raised as an orphan by his grandfather and later by his wealthy uncle, Abu Talib.[46]

Muhammad went through the life of an ordinary Qureshi boy but was exposed to merchant trade by his uncle. He also traveled widely with the trade caravans, including trips to the Mediterranean Sea and the Indian Ocean.

When he reached 25, Mohammad married a wealthy widower called Khadija.[47]

When Muhammad reached 40, he started feeling anxious about life in general. He would spend much time with his family in the hills on the outskirts of Mecca. Then, one night in 610 CE, the angel Gabriel appeared before him in a cave at Mount Jabal al-Nour.

The Angel Gabriel revealed a message from God, *Allah*, which he asked Muhammad to recite. Initially, Muhammad was unable to recite the message. But he could recite the message on the angel's third prompting.

Muhammad recounted the event to Khadija and his close friend Abu Bakr (the Sunni Muslims consider Abu Bakr the successor of Muhammad).[48,49]

Muhammad received other messages from God through the angel Gabriel for 23 years. Muhammad's close acquaintances recorded the messages in the Quran. Indeed, the literal translation of the word Quran is "recitation."[50]

Recognizing the need for a unified scripture, Muhammad's son-in-law, Caliph Uthman, undertook the monumental task of reviewing all the different versions of the Quran. His efforts resulted in the creation of one definitive compilation, known as Uthman's codex, a significant milestone in the history of Islam.[51]

Muhammad spent the rest of his life propagating the messages he received from God via the angel Gabriel.[52]

In the initial stages of his prophetic work, Muhammad encountered tremendous resistance, particularly from the traders of Mecca, who believed in multiple gods. These traders saw Muhammad as a significant threat to their commerce in Mecca, where they thrived and prayed to many gods. Some traders even plotted to murder Muhammad, but he was lucky to escape. He continued to spread the word of Allah from his new base in Medina, which was known as Yathrib.[53]

◆◆◆

The Quran was originally written in Arabic. It is slightly shorter than the Old Testament in the Bible. It is divided into 114 chapters, called *surahs*, grouped into 30 equal sections. The longer *surahs* appear at the front of the book, and the shorter ones at the back. The *surahs* are not in chronological order.[54,55]

Each *surah* has a name. For example, the first *surah* is *Al-Fatihah* (the Opening); the second *surah* is *Al-Bakarah* (the Cow).[56]

Every *surah* (except the first and the ninth) begins with the words "*Bismillahir Rahmani Raheem,*" which means "In the name of Allah the most merciful and the most kind." Also, each *surah* is divided into several verses (*ayah*; plural, *ayat*). The whole Quran contains 6,236 *ayat*.[57]

Before touching the Quran, Muslims must perform certain ablution rights (*wudu*), including washing their hands and feet to be pure before handling it.[58]

Because of its sacredness, the Quran should not be placed on the floor. It should always be kept at a high level. And if on a bookshelf, it should be placed above all other books.[59,60]

The Quran is in Arabic and is read from back to front. The text is read from right to left. Muslims use the Quran to pray to Allah five times a day. The Quran is recited in Arabic during prayers.[61]

The Hadith

The Hadith is a collection of stories about how Prophet Muhammad lived his life. The word "hadith" literally means a narrative, in this instance, a narration of Muhammad's life. His followers compiled it over generations after his death.

The contents of the Hadith can be classified into three categories: a statement of the prophet Muhammad, an action of the prophet Muhammad, and, thirdly, Muhammad's approval of an act done by someone other than him. There are thousands of Hadiths contained in thousands of books.[62]

The Hadith has been used as the source of Islamic law and guidance on the moral conduct of Muslims. The bulk of Sharia law is derived from the Hadith.

The Hadith covers all aspects of life, including how to pray, greet others, and the like.

However, it is worth noting that there is no unanimity amongst Islam followers about the validity of all the Hadith. Some Muslims, such as Ahmed Ibn Hanbal (780–855 CE), consider some hadith as fabrications.[63,64] Other Muslim scholars even go as far as stating that the entire Hadith is not valid, citing chapter 31 surah 6 of the Quran to prove their point:

Among the people, there are those who uphold baseless Hadith, and thus divert others from the path of God without knowledge, and take it in vain. These have incurred a shameful retribution.[65]

Some scholars cite various Hadith verses that seem entirely out of place. Below are a few examples from Submission.org.[66]

> "A group of people from the Oreyneh and Oqayelh tribes came to the prophet to embrace Islam; the prophet advised them to drink the urine of the camels. Later on when they killed the prophet's shepherd, the prophet seized them, gouged out their eyes, cut their hands and legs, and left them thirsty in the desert to die." (Sahih Bukhary; and Hanbel. Bukhary, Volume 1, Book 4, Number 234)

> "If a monkey, a black dog, or a woman passes in front of a praying person, his prayer is nullified." (Sahih Bukhary 8/102 and Hanbel 4/86)

> The prophet said, " Yawning is from Satan. If you are about to yawn, you should try to stop it as much as possible. If you yawn, Satan will laugh." (Sahih Bukhary and Sahih Moslem; Abu Hurayra)

We will revisit this subject in later chapters.

The Sunnah

The Sunnah describes the norms that followers of Islam should adhere to daily. *Sunnah* means "tradition." The Sunnah is the primary source of Sharia law. Sunnah means "mode of life, behavior, or example." It refers to the customs of a community, as opposed to Hadith, which relates to messages that Muhammad communicated orally.

Joseph A. Islam states that a custom described in the Hadith may qualify as a Sunnah. Still, it does not follow that a Hadith may necessarily support a Sunnah.[67]

There is no Islamic book called the Sunnah, but the Sunnah can be said to be embedded in the Hadith literature.

Core Beliefs of Muslims

The fundamental beliefs of the followers of Islam can be divided into six components.[68]

Firstly, Muslims believe that there is only one God, *Allah*, the supreme creator of everything. Further, *Allah* has no equal, nor does Allah have children or parents.

Followers of Islam are required to observe the will of Allah as articulated by his prophet Muhammad and codified in the Quran. Indeed, the followers of Islam believe that the Quran is the word of God Himself. Further, God can be approached through prayer and recitation of the Quran.

The second major component of Muslim beliefs is that there are angels who are God's messengers. The angel Gabriel (Jibril) delivered God's messages to Muhammad, later transcribed into the Quran.

Thirdly, Muslims believe in the holiness of the Quran, which they consider the sacred word of God revealed to the prophet Muhammad.

Fourthly, Muslims believe in the prophets described in the Bible, namely, Adam, Abraham (*Ibrahim*), Moses (*Musa*), and David (*Dawud*). Muslims also consider Jesus (*Isa*) one of the Biblical prophets. Further, they believe that Muhammad was the final prophet.

Fifthly, Islam followers believe that a day of Judgement will come when everyone will be judged for their deeds. On that day, a decision will be made about whether one will go to heaven or hell.

Finally, Muslims believe in predestination. In other words, God knows everything that will happen, but everyone has the free will to choose the path they wish to pursue.

Islam teaches respect for all people irrespective of their religious beliefs. This principle is articulated in the sixth *surah* of chapter 109 of the Quran: "To you is your religion, and to me, my religion."[69]

HINDUISM

Hinduism started in the Indus River in India about 4,000 years ago. The religion's name originates from the Indus River. India comes from the same word. Hinduism is an amalgam of several religious beliefs and practices. It has no single scripture, no single founder, or a standard set of teachings. Hindus worship in a Mandir.

The Sacred Hindu Books

Followers of Hinduism use four holy books: the Vedas, the Ramayana, the Mahabharata, and the Puranas. The Vedas (knowledge) are a compilation of hymns praising the Vedic gods. On the other hand, the Ramayana is a collection of poems on Rama and Sita. The *Mahabharata* is an ancient Sanskrit epic. It includes the *Bhagavad Gita*. The *Puranas* contain stories of various saints.

The Vedas

The Vedas are the oldest sacred Hindu texts, dating back to 1700 BCE. They were written in Sanskrit.

There are four Vedas: *Rig Veda*, *Sama Veda*, *Yajur Veda*, and *Atharva Veda*.[70]

The Rig Veda is a compilation of songs about reality, the universe, and the truth. It also includes songs about wars, weddings, and rituals.[71]

The Yajur Veda covers various types of ceremonies and sacrifices.

The Sama Veda ("a sweet song that removes sorrow") is a compilation of hymns praising the many Hindu gods. The hymns in Veda are usually accompanied by musical instrumentation. Some of the hymns are repetitions of the songs in the Rig Veda. Priests typically use the hymns during the Soma sacrifice.[72]

The Atharva Veda, written much later than the other three Vedas, contains a compilation of procedures for daily life, including curses and spells that can be used to accomplish specific purposes.[73]

The Upanishads

The Upanishads date back to around 800 BCE. They are philosophical texts that question some things mentioned in the Vedas. The Upanishads describe how the "soul (*Atman*) can be united with Brahman's ultimate truth through meditation and contemplation."[74]

The Puranas

There are 18 Puranas, divided into three parts named after the Hindu deities Brahma, Vishnu, and Shiva. These sacred books cover the history of the creation of the universe and describe the kings and heroes of Hindu culture.[75]

The Mahabharata

The Mahabharata, written by the sage Vyasa around the 4th century BCE, is the longest poem ever written. It is about five times the length of the Bible.[76]

The poem contains legends of the Bharatas, a story full of intrigue, drama, love, hate, and other earthly passions. The underlying message is that we should live a life that ensures we realize our Dharma (the proper behavior and social order) so that the universe can achieve Dharma, too.[77]

The Bhagavad Gita

The Bhagavad Gita is a crucial divine document of the Hindus. The text is sometimes referred to as the Gita. It is considered the sixth book of the Mahabharata, dating back to 300 BCE. Hindu scholars attribute the authorship of the Gita to Vyasa, the author of the Mahabharata.

The Gita contains a philosophical conversation between the warrior Arjuna and the god Krishna. It inspires Hindus to live a life that will ensure the full realization of Dharma.

Many Hindus consider Gita essential reading for anyone interested in the Hindu religion.[78]

The world's largest copy of the Gita weighs 800 kg and measures more than 2.8 meters. It is located in Delhi at the Sri Sri Radha Parthasarathi Mandir (the ISKCON Temple).

The Ramayana

The Ramayana, written by the poet Valmiki in 1 BCE, is based on oral traditions dating back to 7 BCE. It is an epic love story that describes the life of Prince Rama—a captivating story about how his wife was abducted and how he fought with demons.[79]

Core Beliefs of the Hindus

Hinduism has seven core beliefs.[80] Firstly, Hindus believe in one universal soul called Brahman.

Secondly, they believe in the immortality of the individual soul called *Atman*. In other words, your soul does not disappear once you depart from this earth. It emerges again in a new life after death - the phenomenon known as transmigration.

Thirdly, Hindus believe in Karma, which refers to the good or bad actions that impact society. The underlying idea is that one's actions today will affect one's new life after death. Similarly, one's past actions in an earlier life affect one's present life. This Karma cycle is everlasting. It can only be broken by performing certain Hindu rituals, the subject of the fourth belief.

Fourthly, Hindus believe that the cycle of good or bad Karma can be broken by *Moksha* (liberation from the cycle of birth, death, and rebirth), reaching a personal realization of oneness with Brahman.

Fifthly, Hindus believe in the Vedas, the Hindu sacred books, the Rig Veda, the Sama Veda, the Yajur Veda, and the Atharva Veda.

Sixthly, Hindus believe in the cyclical nature of time. In other words, there is no beginning or end to time. Further, time is divided into four epochs (Yuga) that repeat thousands of years. The epochs are Krita Yuga (1,728,000 years), Treta Yuga (1,296,000 years), Dvapara Yuga (864,000 years), and *Kali Yuga (432,000 years)*. The complete cycle takes 4,320,000 years. We are in the Kali epoch, which started on February 18, 3102 BCE.

Finally, Hindus believe in *Dharma*, the right way of living. The underlying idea is that all human beings and all living things need to maintain their Dharma to ensure the right balance in the world. If one does not preserve their Dharma, an imbalance will emerge, with unpleasant consequences.

Hindus believe that one must aim at four goals in their life. These are Dharma, a well-balanced life; Artha, the pursuit of prosperity; Kama Sutra, the pursuit of mental and bodily pleasure; and Moksha, breaking the cycle of life and death.

Hindus also believe that one should avoid lust for material possessions (*Kama*), anger (*Khrona*), and greed (*Lobha*). Also, attachment to things, people, and power (*Moha*), pride (*Mada*), and jealousy (*Matsaharya*). By following these edicts, a person can achieve Moksha and realize Dharma.

The other unique feature of Hinduism compared to Christianity and Islam is that Hindus believe in thousands of gods. For example, they believe in *Brahma*, the creator of everything on earth. Saraswati, the God of learning, and Vishnu, the preserver of the world, created by Brahma until Shiva eventually destroys it. Vishnu has several Avatars, including Rama and Krishna, who work as his defenders of Dharma on earth. He has two consorts, too, the goddesses *Lakshmi* and *Bhu Devi*. The third member of the Hindu Trinity is Shiva, the destroyer. Shiva prepares the world for destruction at the end of each cycle, for renewal into a new world. There are many other gods.

Hinduism has four main denominations: the Vaishnavas, who worship God Vishnu; the Shaivas, who worship Shiva; the Smartas, who focus on the sacred texts: the Puranas, the Ramayana, and the Mahabharata. They do not use the Vedas. They worship five goddesses. Finally, there are the *Shaktas*, who worship the goddess, Devi.

Hindus also believe that when evil increases substantially, it begins to tip the balance in Dharma. When this happens, Avatar intervenes to address the situation. Avatars are gods that descend on Earth to help restore order.

Hindus also have a caste system that has received attention worldwide. The caste system is based on the Bhagavad Gita and the Rig Veda. According to this system, people are born into different castes based on a hierarchy of importance.

At the top of the hierarchy are the *Brahmins* (priests). The *Kshatriyas* (warriors) are at the next level, and the Vaishyas (traders) are below. On the next level down are the *Shudras* (laborers).

The Rig Veda states that God Parusha created human beings. The *Brahmin* were created from the face of Parusha, *Kshatriyas* from the arms, the *Vaishyas* from the thighs, and the *Shudras* from the feet.

The classification of people into these four categories was initially based on their abilities, not their birth. Indeed, people could move between the four classes in the early years depending on their skills. However, around 8 BCE, the Laws of Manu (also known as the *Manusmrti*) were introduced, creating rules that forbade movement between the castes. One had to remain in the caste in which they were born. Over time, the people without caste were considered the lowest of the low. Accordingly, they were destined for the worst jobs, such as cleaning toilets. They became known as the *untouchables*.

Many people consider the caste system discriminatory, mainly because people are born into a caste. It is not a matter of personal choice. The system is gradually waning with the modernization of society.

BUDDHISM

Buddhism was started by Siddhartha Gautama (563 – 410 BCE) as an offshoot of the Brahmin wing of the Hindu religion. Siddhartha Gautama was unhappy about some teachings of Hinduism, notably the caste system, which he felt was discriminatory. Accordingly, he set up his religion, which everyone could join, regardless of their caste. He also opposed the Vedic scriptures, including the sacrifices the Vedas prescribed.

Gautama was brought up in a relatively privileged home. However, when he reached 29, he became disenchanted with that lifestyle and experienced vast emptiness. He renounced all earthly possessions and embarked on a journey of self-discovery. He started doing yoga and lived a frugal life. He abstained from all worldly desires. When he reached self-enlightenment, he began preaching about the enlightenment he had seen. He established a monastery of followers called the *sangha*.

Unlike Christianity, Islam, and Hinduism, which have sacred religious texts, Buddhism does not have such texts. Gautama's teachings were mainly oral, but his followers later documented these oral teachings in the *Tipitaka*.

The Tipitaka

The Tipitaka is believed to have been composed around 500 BCE and handed down orally through several generations. Its codification into written manuscripts was done around 1 BCE, during the reign of King Walagambahu of Sri Lanka, 500 hundred years after the death of the founder of Buddhism, Gautama Budha.[81]

Tipitaka means "three baskets." It represents the three sections into which Buddha's followers codified his teachings around 1 BCE.

The three parts are the *Sutta Pitaka*, a collection of dialogues between Buddha and other people; the *Vinaya Pitaka*, the code of monastic discipline; and the *Abhidharma Pitaka*, which contains the Buddhist philosophy, psychology, and various doctrines.

The *Sutta Piṭaka* contains more than 10,000 *suttas* (rules) Buddhists in monasteries must follow daily. These rules include things like the mode of dress.

The *Vinaya Pitaka*, on the other hand, is like a code of conduct for Buddhist monks and nuns. It contains around 225 rules that are supposed to govern the behavior of Buddhist monks and nuns.

The *Abhidharma Pitaka* systematically analyzes the other two books and represents the essence of Buddhist doctrines.[82, 83]

The Tipitaka is approximately 11 times the size of the Bible.[84]

Core Beliefs of Buddhists

Buddhists believe in the Four Noble Truths. First, life involves suffering, from birth to death and even after death, in the cyclical progression of time, as taught in Hinduism.[85]

Secondly, suffering is brought about by a lack of understanding of the nature of reality and the desires that emanate from that lack of knowledge.[86]

Thirdly, suffering can be eliminated by removing the desires and attachment to material possessions.[87]

Fourthly, wisdom, morality, and concentration are the path to enlightenment. This encompasses the right views, intention, speech, action, livelihood, effort, right-mindedness, and contemplation.[88]

Three fundamental principles or doctrines are linked to the 8-point path: *Anatman*, *Karma*, and *Nirvana*.[89]

Anatman means the denial of the permanent soul. According to Buddha, an individual exists in a state of instability based on five aspects of existence: the material body, feelings, perceptions, karmic tendencies, and consciousness. Based on this principle, Buddhists believe that nobody stays the same from one moment to another. Everyone is constantly changing.[90]

Karma, on the other hand, is the doctrine that deals with the ethical consequences of one's actions. In other words, good deeds are ultimately rewarded with good. In contrast, evil deeds are rewarded with bad – what has been described by some scholars as universal justice.

According to Buddha, "karma of varying types can lead to rebirth as a human, an animal, a hungry ghost, a denizen of hell, or even one of the Hindu gods." The vital point is that Buddhism does not prescribe rules one should follow to sustain good karma. One is expected to live an ethical life that ultimately produces good karma.[91]

The doctrine of Nirvana states that the goal of living the life of a good Buddhist is to escape from the cycle of suffering and achieve the utmost enlightenment, free of greed, hatred, and ignorance—to attain a state of *nirvana*. The Buddhists believe that after achieving nirvana, one should sustain it until death—the final *nirvana* called *parinirvana*.[92]

Buddhists believe the journey toward nirvana is an inner journey cultivated through virtuous living that involves loving-kindness, compassion, sympathetic joy, and equanimity. These four virtues are described as the Palaces of Brahma. These virtues entail ethically fulfilling one's duties to society, being charitable, and adhering to the five moral principles of Buddhism: prohibition of killing, stealing, harmful language, sexual misbehavior, and intoxication.[93]

Buddhism is divided into two denominations: *Theravada* (the Way of the Elders) and *Mahayana* (the Great Vehicle).[94]

Part Two

Religion, Culture, and Science

Chapter 5

Religion and Culture

*"Wherever the African is, there is
religion."*
—John Mbiti

IT IS DIFFICULT TO DISENTANGLE religion from culture. The two are intertwined in complex ways, and it is sometimes difficult to tell whether religion is a subset of culture or vice versa. We will, therefore, start our journey by looking at a working definition of culture. We will then look at examples of cultural practices that directly conflict with religious practices. This will help us understand the complex dynamics one sometimes has to wade through in seeking spiritual enlightenment.

What is Culture?

There are many definitions of culture. I prefer the one I learned in high school. It states that culture is a way of life fashioned by people to come to terms with their environment. In other words, culture encompasses the set of beliefs and values a particular community has developed over time that serve as guardrails in their daily lives as they engage amongst themselves, with other communities, and with the environment. Culture is multi-layered. It includes language, music, social habits, what people wear, how they wear it, religion, and other aspects of life that give the community an identity.[95] This will be our perspective of culture as we explore the question of religion versus culture.

It would also be helpful to recap our understanding of religion. Religion can be found in all human cultures in different shapes and forms. The key components of religion are "n. 1 belief in a personal God or gods entitled to obedience and worship 2 expression of this in worship 3 particular system of faith and worship 4 thing that one is devoted to".[96]

Religious beliefs subsist within a particular cultural environment. And the same religion can be practiced in different ways in different cultures.

Religion and culture can be better understood by considering that many people follow certain religions, not because they made a personal choice but because their communities chose it through a gradual adaptation process.

For example, I became a Christian through induction into my parents' faith as a child. Most people in my community were followers of the Christian faith.

◆◆◆

Johann Ludwig Krapf, a German Lutheran missionary, introduced Christianity in Kenya in 1844. Johannes Rebmann joined him a little later, and in 1846, they jointly started the Church Missionary Society (CMS) station in Rabai, near Mombasa.

The religion gradually became entrenched in the community. Over time, many Kenyans accepted it. It became part of the fabric of the local culture, albeit in differing degrees across the country.

Christianity greatly enriched the lives of the local communities by introducing schools, healthcare systems, and improved agricultural practices introduced by the missionaries.

However, people continued with other traditional practices even after embracing the new religion. For example, the conventions for naming children, the traditional marriage procedures and ceremonies, and so forth continued. It was indeed an interesting blend of cultural practices.

A brief literature review of cultural and religious practices in different parts of the world reveals several complex dynamics. We will explore a few examples to appreciate the depths to which some of the schisms between traditional cultural practices and religion reached.

EXAMPLES OF ANTAGONISM BETWEEN TRADITIONAL CULTURAL PRACTICES AND RELIGIOUS PRACTICES

The Taliban of Afghanistan

Taliban (which means "students" in Pashto, Afghanistan's official language) was formed in the early 1990s. Mohammed Omar and Abdul Ghani Baradar founded the movement after Soviet Union troops, who had been fighting the US–Saudi–Pakistan-supported Islamic *mujahedeen,* left Afghanistan.[97] The movement was started in Sunni Islam seminaries in the Pashtun area, which covers parts of Pakistan and Afghanistan. Saudi Arabia sponsored the seminaries.[98]

The main aim of the Taliban was to secure peace and security for the Afghan people and introduce Islamic law.[99]

The Taliban came into power in Afghanistan in 1996 after overthrowing President Burhanuddin Rabbani. After taking over control, the Taliban introduced their strict version of *Sharia* law. However, this created challenges because judges could apply the law based on their interpretation of *Sharia.* The muddle sometimes led to Mullah Omar, a self-proclaimed *amir al muminin* or commander of the believers, making the final legal decisions."[100]

The Taliban introduced other oppressive laws in the name of Islam. For example, they did not allow women to be educated. Also, women were publicly flogged for failing to wear the traditional dress, going shopping unaccompanied by a male relative, and other minor infractions.[101]

The Taliban also banned various pastimes they considered "un-Islamic." They banned television, music, and cinema. They also banned flying kites, dog fights, and *buzkashi* (a traditional sport played on horseback where the objective is to place a headless, dismembered goat in a goal). On the other hand, they allowed soccer, cricket, volleyball, and boxing.[102]

The Taliban destroyed other elements of traditional Afghanistan life, including two giant Buddha of Bamiyan statues, which caused outrage worldwide. The Taliban considered such images idolatrous.[103]

The Taliban were removed from power in 2001 through military force by a coalition led by the United States of America. However, the Taliban remained active in many parts of Afghanistan and continued to wage an insurgency war. They ceased their military activity in February 2020 after signing a peace deal with the United States of America.[104]

It is incredible to note that a religious organization could cause so much suffering to people and destroy their cultural artifacts.

The Igbo of Nigeria

Background of the Igbo People

The Igbo (also called Ibo) are the third-largest ethnic group in Nigeria, with about 32 million or 15.2% of the population. They live primarily in the south-central and southeastern parts of Nigeria.

There are differing views on the origin and meaning of "Igbo." However, "Igbo" in the Igbo language means ancient people.[105]

Traditional Igbo Religious Beliefs

The Igbo traditional religion is deeply rooted in the culture of the Igbo people and resembles Western religions. Key features include beliefs handed down through generations, sacred myths, rituals, and a well-structured hierarchy of elders, kings, priests, and diviners.

The Igbo people believe in a Supreme Being (*Chi-ukwu*) whose abord is in the sky, where he controls the whole world. Multiple other names in Igbo refer to the Supreme Being (God). The names include Chineke (Creator), *Eze enu* (King of Heaven), *Osebuluwa* (Lord who upholds the world), and so forth.[106] The Igbo God is ubiquitous, invisible, and the fountain of justice. He is also transcendental and incomprehensible.[107,108]

The Igbo also believe in lesser deities (*Alusi*) who are messengers of *Chukwu* (God). These lesser deities manifest themselves in the Igbo people's day-to-day activities.[109] These deities include *Idemili*, the god of water, *Ufiejioku*, the god of agriculture, and others.[110]

There are other personalized gods, such as *Chi*, who control the luck of an individual.[111]

Other features of the Igbo traditional religion include the worship of ancestors, who they believe are the guardians of morality. They also believe in the concepts of *ofo* and *ogu*, which symbolize justice, righteousness, and truth. The Igbo people also believe in the sacredness of the earth, as manifested in their worship of *Ala*, the earth deity.[112]

Similar to the Hindus, the Igbo people believe in reincarnation. However, unlike the Hindus, the Igbos believe that reincarnation only applies to those who do good deeds during their lifetime. Sinful people, on the other hand, transform into spirits.[113]

The Advent of Christianity in Igbo Land

Christianity was started in Nigeria in 1842 by Reverend Thomas Birth Freeman, a Methodist missionary. Reverend Schon introduced it to Igbo land in 1857.[114] Despite initial resistance from the Igbo people, who felt that Christianity would destroy their local culture, Christianity started gaining traction. The church won converts through church-school teachers called church agents.

The missionaries built schools and churches, which they used to attract children and youth to Christianity.[115]

The Emergence of Antagonism

After some time, the Igbo people started conflicting with the missionaries. The scenario is aptly described by Okeke, Ibemwa, and Okeke (2017):

At different times and places, there were face-to-face encounter[s] with Christians and traditionalists because the early Christian missionaries behaved like social revolutionaries. They plunged into the condemnation and eradication of traditional religion. Traditional music and song, drama, and dance were totally denounced as bad and immoral. Statues, images, and emblems of remarkable artistic work and aesthetic merit were wantonly destroyed by some of the overzealous converts as idols and works of the devil. The missionaries were not prepared to face traditional religion. These acts set the stage for conflicts, which soon ensued between the Christians and the traditionalists.[116]

The antagonism between the Igbo people and the Christians was quite significant. One manifestation of this rift was the destruction of traditional shrines and sacred groves. Also, customary naming rights for children became a source of conflict, forcing some traditionalists to coerce Christians to perform the traditional naming rights.

Also, Christians opposed the initiation rites customarily performed to mark the transition from puberty. The Christians considered such rights as heathenish and ungodly.

The differences ran into marriage and burial rites, too. Christians found some traditional burial practices unacceptable. For example, in the olden days, important people in the community, such as chiefs, were buried with gold, money, other ornaments, and live people to escort them to the land of the spirits. The deceased person's wife was also required to perform rites that appeared quite obnoxious, such as crawling over the husband's corpse and staying for 28 days without a bath.[117]

It would appear that the antagonism between the Igbo traditionalists and Christians will continue until there is a dialogue between the two parties. Certain practices are similar, while others may need to be abandoned to facilitate harmonious coexistence.

The Kikuyu of Kenya

This example relates to schisms between the Kikuyu people of Kenya and the Presbyterian Church of East Africa (PCEA), one of the largest Christian church organizations in the region inhabited by the Kikuyu. The schisms concerned the circumcision of girls (*irua*) and the traditional rites of passage for accepting a man into different levels of elderhood by joining the tribal governance body called *kiama*.

First, we will briefly examine the background of the Kikuyu cultural practices in question and the PCEA Church.

Contentious Kikuyu Cultural Practices

Female Circumcision

For a long time, the circumcision of boys and girls (*irua*) was an important event in the traditional culture of the Kikuyu people. Circumcision marked the initiation of boys and girls into mature adults who could marry, beget children, and engage in other activities in the community—in the case of the man, attaining the essential qualification to seek admission into certain tribal administration groups.[118] *Irua* was, in effect, the rite of passage from adolescence to adulthood.

People who were circumcised at the same time formed a permanent bond that would remain for the rest of their lives. Such people were known as people of the same "*rika*" (age group). The *rika* was given a name that reflected an important contemporary event during the circumcision.

The *rika* was an essential mark in the history of the Kikuyu people.[119]

In the case of the males, circumcision was a minor, albeit painful, procedure. During circumcision, it was expected that the boy would not even flinch as a sign of courage.[120]

In the case of the females, the surgical procedure was slightly more intrusive. (It was mainly the Type II clitorectomy, according to the World Health Organization classification).[121] Despite the apparently gruesome operation, it was an accepted practice in the Kikuyu community before the advent of the Christian missionaries.[122]

Female circumcision was considered an essential rite of passage in the Kikuyu tradition.

It was considered taboo for a Kikuyu man to marry an uncircumcised girl. Similarly, it was almost unheard of for a circumcised woman to marry an uncircumcised man. These customs were enforced rigidly until the cultural practice was overtaken by modernization and prohibited by Kenyan law in 2011.[123]

Kiama

The Kikuyu people have a rich cultural heritage, described in Jomo Kenyatta's book Facing Mount Kenya.[124] One of the key aspects of traditional Kikuyu culture is an elaborate system of government. The system dates back to the period before the advent of the colonial government and the missionaries. According to Kikuyu tradition, the government was initially run by a leader called Gikuyu. There was no democracy during his reign.

After some time, the Kikuyu people revolted and overthrew Gikuyu's government. A new government was promulgated in a big ceremony called "*itwika*" around 1892 – 1898.

During that "*itwika*" ceremony, it was agreed that all members of the Kikuyu tribe would be involved in the government subsequently. For practical purposes, the tribe would be divided into two ruling classes, Mwangi and Maina (or Irungu). One class would rule for approximately 40 years, then hand over the reins to the other. The mantle was handed to Mwangi during that initial ceremony.

Additionally, the tribe agreed to follow nine rules for governing the tribe. The rules included a declaration that every member of the community who became circumcised would be entitled to participate in the tribal government. Also, circumcised women would have the same political status in the tribe as circumcised men.

Additionally, the government would be constituted by a council of elders, *kiama*. Membership in the *kiama* would be restricted to married men with an established homestead.

There were three categories of eldership. The lowest rank was *kiama kia kamatimu* (council of warriors). The next in the hierarchy was *kiama kia mataathi* (council of peace). The highest rank was *kiama kia maturanguru* (religious and sacrificial council).

To join any of these levels of *kiama*, an elder had to fulfill certain requirements. For example, to join *kiama kia kamatimu*, the elder was required to pay one *mburi* (goat or sheep). The role of the *kamatimu* elders included performing mundane tasks during assemblies of the *kiama*, such as skinning *mburi* and lighting fire to roast the *mburi*.

To join *kiama kia mataathi*, an elder was required to have a son or daughter who had reached the age of circumcision. An elaborate ceremony called *gutonyio kirira* would be performed at the elder's homestead, presided over by seasoned elders of the *kiama*. At the ceremony's climax, a goat (a male goat in this instance) would be slaughtered and used to perform certain traditional rituals, symbolizing the elder's acceptance as a peacemaker in the community. The ritual would be followed by a big celebration during which the elders would feast on meat, beer, and other food. The ceremony would also involve singing ceremonial songs and dancing by the elders and their wives.

To join the highest and most honored *kiama kia maturanguru*, it was a requirement that all the candidate's children should have been circumcised. Also, the candidate's wife should have passed childbearing age. The candidate was also required to make a payment in the form of an ewe (full-grown female sheep). The ewe was slaughtered and used in a ceremony performed by the *kiama kia maturanguru* elders under the sacred *mugumo* tree. Only members of the *kiama kia maturanguru* were allowed to participate in this ceremony. The primary purpose of the ceremony was to dedicate the life of the newly appointed *maturanguru* elder to God (*Ngai*) and the community's welfare.

The elders of the *kiama kia maturanguru* were the high priests of the Kikuyu traditional society. They were the ones who performed the religious and ethical ceremonies of the community.

Regarding God (*Ngai*), Kenyatta points out that:

The Gikuyu believe in one God, Ngai, the creator and giver of all things. He has no father, mother, or companion of any kind. His work is done in solitude. He loves or hates people according to their behavior. The creator lives in the sky but has temporary homes on earth, situated on mountains, where he may rest during his visits. The visits are made with a view to his carrying out a kind of "general inspection" and to bring blessings and punishments to the people.[125]

◆◆◆

The cultural practices described above started changing gradually due to the influence of Western religion and modernization.

The practices are now on the rise, although not performed in the strict traditional way. The essential elements of admission and transition within the different *kiama* hierarchy have remained almost intact. Also, elders initiated into the *kiama* continue to play various traditional roles in the Kikuyu community. In particular, members of *kiama* are typically involved in dowry negotiations and organizing circumcision ceremonies for boys (jointly with the church in many instances).[126]

The elders of *kiama* also play a role in mediating family disputes. They have also been actively propagating knowledge of Kikuyu culture in different fora, including local radio and television stations.

Many adherents of the Kikuyu *kiama* cultural practices do not see any conflict between the *kiama* system and Christianity. They see the *kiama* as complimentary to the church in promoting the moral virtues of the Kikuyu community and worshiping the one known God (*Ngai*).[127] Indeed, many Kikuyu elders who are members of *kiama* are also staunch members of the Christian church, including the PCEA church (based on my knowledge).

The Presbyterian Church of East Africa

The Presbyterian Church of East Africa (PCEA) has existed for over 100 years. Its origin is unique. It was started by missionaries from Scotland in 1891 under the sponsorship of directors of the Imperial British East Africa Chartered Company. The directors were Sir William Mackinnon (the company's founder), A.L. Bruce, and others. They wanted to start a Scottish Mission in the Maasai, Kamba, and Kikuyu communities.[128]

The church was started by Dr. James Stewart in temporary quarters at Kibwezi in Ukambani in 1892. It was initially known as the East African Scottish Mission. After a while, the church started looking for an alternative location. This was due to malaria at Kibwezi, which had killed some missionaries.

The church moved to Kikuyu, in Central Kenya, in 1898 and reconstituted itself as the Church of Scotland Mission (CMS). The church expanded to other parts of Central Kenya, including Chuka, Mwimbi, Imenti, and Chogoria. It became one of the largest missionary churches in Kikuyu land.

Philip Karanja was the first African baptized in the church in 1907.[129] By 1910, the church had 53 members. The church's first African pastors were ordained in 1926: Rev. Musa Gitau, Reverend Benjamin Githieya, and Reverend Joshua Matenjwa.

The church expanded into other parts of the country, reaching more than 4 million members in 2020. Today, the church leadership is comprised of Africans.[130]

The PCEA has become one of the largest churches within the Kikuyu community. It has been pursuing aggressive expansion strategies to entrench itself in people's lives.

Role of the PCEA Church in the Community

The PCEA church has been an important institution within the Kikuyu community and the country. The church has been involved in community development since the early 1890s. For example, a Scottish missionary, John Paterson, introduced basic agricultural practices and the first coffee seeds in 1893.[131] Coffee became a significant cash crop in Kenya several decades later, particularly in Kikuyu land. Coffee is now the country's fifth largest foreign exchange earner after tea, tourism, diaspora remittances, and horticulture. Coffee is grown in 33 out of the 47 counties in the country by more than 800,000 smallholder farmers and 3,000 estates. The coffee sector currently employs about six million people.[132]

Today, the church is involved in multiple community development activities in Kikuyu land and other parts of the country. These activities include providing spiritual nourishment to more than 1,000 congregations.

The church also sponsors numerous community projects, such as hospitals, health centers, schools, schools for the deaf, schools for impoverished children, old people's homes, and many others. The church is fully entrenched in the local community, especially the Kikuyu community.[133]

But, as the Kikuyu proverb says, *mathanwa mari kiondo kimwe matiagaga gukomorania* (axes in one basket must hit against each other), as is evident from the controversies that have emerged between the PCEA church and the Kikuyu people from time to time.

Controversy Regarding Female Circumcision

In the late 1920s, there was a controversy in the church regarding the practice of female circumcision. The church felt that the practice was immoral, barbaric, and wrong from a medical perspective. It discouraged its members from engaging in the practice. This caused a significant rift within the church. Some members who disagreed with the church left and set up their denominations. The viciousness of the controversy was extraordinary.[134]

Dr. John Arthur of the Church of Scotland started the campaign to abolish the practice as early as 1906. It continued simmering in the background for several years. In 1928, the Kikuyu Central Association announced that they would contest elections for positions in the Native Council on the platform of preserving Kikuyu culture, including female circumcision.

Shortly after that, the church in Tumutumu asked its baptized members to declare their loyalty to the church by opposing the practice. The church even stopped referring to the practice as circumcision. Instead, the church called it "sexual mutilation of women."

In an unfortunate incident at Kijabe in January 1930, a church missionary named Hulda Stumpf was murdered, allegedly for her strong views against the practice. The matter went to court, but nobody was convicted because of a lack of evidence.

Children of Kikuyu people who did not denounce the practice were prevented from attending schools run by the missionaries. This caused an uproar. People called upon the government to address the situation.

The ban was lifted, but only teachers who had denounced the practice were allowed to teach in the schools. However, this compromise did not assuage the feelings of the Kikuyu protagonists.

There was a call for the establishment of independent schools. The result was the formation of independent Gikuyu and Karenga schools completely free of missionaries in education and religious matters. But the matter did not end there.[135]

Agitation for the abolition of the practice continued to grow. The matter was even brought up for debate in the House of Commons in the UK. A committee set up to investigate the matter decided that the best way of dealing with the issue was through the education of the local communities rather than using force to bring about change.

In other words, giving people the correct information and letting them make independent choices.[136]

The strong sentiments of the Kikuyu traditionalists on this subject can be gleaned from the words of Jomo Kenyatta.

> *The real argument lies not in defense of the surgical operation or its details but in the understanding of a very important fact in the tribal psychology of the Gikuyu—namely, that this operation is still regarded as the very essence of an institution which has enormous educational, social, moral and religious implications, quite apart from the operation itself. For the present it is impossible for a member of the tribe to imagine an initiation without clitoridectomy. Therefore the abolition of the surgical element in this custom means to the Gikuyu the abolition of the whole institution.*[137]

The issue raged for years, spearheaded by United Nations agencies and multiple human rights organizations worldwide.

In Kenya, the practice was forbidden with the passage of the Children's Act in 2001. The Act made it a criminal offense to carry out circumcision of any girl under 18. The law was tightened even further with the enactment of the Prohibition of Female Genital Mutilation Act in 2011. This legislation prohibited circumcision of women of any age, with a penalty of up to seven years in prison for violating the law.

Today, there appears to be unanimity within the Kikuyu community that the practice is improper and abhorrent to modern civilized life.

Controversy Regarding Kiama

Following a meeting of the General Assembly of the PCEA (the supreme governing body of the church) held at the St. Andrews Church, Nairobi, in the second week of April 2018, a letter was sent to all the PCEA churches in Kenya asking congregants to keep away from the traditional Kikuyu practices of "*mburi cia kiama*."[138,139,140] The communication regarding this subject also appeared in a post on the PCEA Facebook page on May 22, 2018. The message read as follows:

> *#GA(General #Assembly); #ifikiemoderator, the highest body in PCEA church, has distanced with #MburiCiaKiama, terming it as a negative cultural practice amongst other practices like polygamous practice, female circumcision, and witchcraft. Is it right for a Christian to give Mburi Cia Kiama? Great talk indeed,*
> *Have we embraced #traditional god as Christians??*
> *Is this idol worshipping? (worshipping more than one god)*
> *Since you do not think it worth to retain the knowledge of God. The consequence of idol worship [is] very clear in the Bible; check Romans 1:18-32, among others. Christians will NEVER have two gods. If u get a second one, then you are not a Christian.*

The communication was met with outrage by some members of the Kikuyu community – both members and non-members of the PCEA church. The vitriolic exchange that ensued from both sides of the divide was astonishing. Below are extracts from the Presbyterian Church of East Africa message board on Facebook in May 2018.

<u>Supporters of the Church's Directive</u>

I consider all to be garbage that I may gain Christ! Philippians 3:8 That sums it all! Kikuyu customs are all garbage, for the knowledge of Jesus Christ my Lord. Carnal Christians will never ever comprehend this verse. Only a spiritual Christian will. I am not there yet. It's a journey, so help me, God! (Moses Njuguna)

thanks P.C.E.A for exposing darkness... darkness is darkness. (Pitahx Gachigi)

Kikuyu traditional culture is so backward n gibberish. They believe in the blood of lambs but Christianity believes in the blood of the lamb (George JaKodiere)

<u>Opponents of the Church's Directive</u>

Personally I support the agikuyu elders... PCEA leadership, you have failed.. And I think there are some pressing issues like accountability that you should concentrate on... Always remember we had culture even before the Bible.... That mzungu who brought the Bible has his culture that he follows till today.. Aaaaaai nimwathie muno (Hunja Wa Hunja)

Once you join this pcea thing! Its simple you follow the orders from the above without questioning!!! And then bring money as much as you can to retain your membership!!Otherwise membership is voluntary, so stop threatening members to choose between options dictated by you!!!
Stick to your lane as a church and through your actions others will follow suit!!! #bottomline# stop dictatorship!!!!(Wangechi Ndegwa)

Muthoga Kirethi, the Chairman of the Kikuyu Council of Elders in Nyeri County, was reported in the *Daily Nation* newspaper on May 24, 2018, as having said the following:

> *That is unwarranted and misguided. We do not rival the church by embracing our culture. In fact, we were born Kikuyu first before we joined the mainstream churches. People can opt to leave a church, but you can never stop being Kikuyu.*[141]

The debate continued raging in the local press and other social media platforms. One article that seemed to encapsulate the intense emotions of the anti-PCEA directive appeared in the Daily Nation newspaper on June 2, 2018, written by Ngwiri (2018). Below is a "rather long" extract:

> *Three weeks ago, there was a hue and cry when the church's highest governing body, the General Assembly, declared it was barring its members from participating in a Kikuyu cultural ritual, Mburi cia Kiama, in which male adults donate a goat or two to be eaten by their age-mates as a way of seeking acceptance as tribal elders.*
>
> *The main aim of this simple ritual is to advise men what they should and should not do in their daily lives in terms of observing cultural norms, marriage, and community responsibilities.*
>
> *IDENTITY*
> *The ritual is completely devoid of politics and has nothing to do with worship of any deity or idol.*

What the church leaders seem to oppose most is the symbolic consumption of a traditional Kikuyu brew by elders and initiates alike.

If a man has not undergone it, he is regarded as a boy regardless of his age or marital status and may not participate in activities like negotiating bride price, for instance, which is men's work. As far as I know, nothing in this ceremony should raise the hackles of church leaders.

Historically, there are many practices that the church has, with justification, frowned upon. Among them are polygamy (Lord knows why since a number of clerics, especially married ones, avidly practice serial monogamy), clitoridectomy, witchcraft, homosexuality, and prostitution.

PRACTICES

Such strictures make a great deal of sense if the tribe is to survive with its mores intact. In any case, many such practices – except adultery – are against the law of the land. So why would PCEA leaders go out of their way to ban a harmless ritual?

When did they last speak with such a loud voice against the far worse evils bedeviling this country like runaway corruption, grand theft, tribalism, pedophilia, oppression, and other forms of immorality and crime?

Why should they be worried that grown men are advised against eating certain pieces of meat from a ritually slaughtered goat, venturing into their daughters' bedroom at any one time, or associating too closely with uncircumcised boys?

EVIL
PCEA, which is only four-million strong in Kenya, has had its share of problems which remain unresolved.

Among its adherents are thieves, perverts, witches, and people who see demons at every corner.

Among them too are deacons who murder their wives and devotees who, with their clandestine lovers, plot the destruction of their husbands.

These are the people the church should be concerned about, not how much "muratina" a member drinks once in a lifetime.

With such uncompromising and hypocritical edicts, the church is unlikely to attract many new members who can see through the hypocrisy. [142]

Many of the Kikuyu elders who are members of the controversial *kiamas* are staunch followers of Christianity. Even during the independence struggle in Kenya, the Mau Mau freedom fighters, mainly Kikuyu men and women, embraced Christianity. They believed the Christian God was the same as their ancestors' God (*Ngai*). In other words, there was no separate God for the Africans and another different God for Europeans.

Indeed, the thinking then was that only the names used to refer to God had changed, such as Yahweh, El, Jah, and Elohim.[143]

Based on my experience, the principles of moral conduct taught in Christianity are similar to those of the Kikuyu traditionalists. If the two parties were to engage in dialogue, then perhaps a synergy could emerge whereby the PCEA church would reflect the real character of the Kikuyu traditions. The church would also gain greater acceptance within the Kikuyu community.

Equally, the Kikuyu culture, of which Christianity has become an essential component, would be significantly enriched. This has happened before, albeit in different, less emotive circumstances. An example is the case of the Christian missionary Dr. Crawford, who applied the principles described in the book of Corinthians in the Bible (1 Corinthians 9:22) and demonstrated great respect for the African rituals of baptism, thereby facilitating the acceptance of Christianity among the Embu people, as described by Gathogo:

In particular, Crawford attempted to identify himself with [the] traditional system of government. [In] 1910, he sought to join the Embu Council of Elders with the hope of influencing the society from within. In addition, for his entrance fee, he presented the elders with a bull, and there was a great feast. This made the Embu elders recognize him as one of their own, and his 'religion' as part of theirs.

In turn, they promised him 'that they would now insist on all the people keeping God's Day and attending [church] service and that he was to be the leading elder (Muthamaki).[144]

At the time of writing, the debate is ongoing. Neither party has made serious attempts to reach out to the other for dialogue. If such a dialogue does not occur, the antagonism will likely continue. Each side will hold firmly on to its respective views, occasionally deriding the other in church pulpits, TV, radio, and other fora.

Chapter 6

Religion and Science

*"There isn't nothing to worry about
between science and religion, because
the contradictions are just in your mind.
Of course, they are there, but they are not
in the Lord's mind because He made the
whole thing, so there is a way, if we are
smart enough, to understand them so
that we will not have any
contradictions."*
—Henry Eyring

AS RATIONAL HUMAN BEINGS, THERE are many things we encounter that do not seem to make sense. Scientists have periodically tried to answer our questions regarding the workings of the physical world. However, the truth is that even the most sophisticated and highly acclaimed scientific explanations of physical phenomena are incomplete.

For example, we know that to calculate the area of a circle, we must multiply its radius by the number 2 and by the ratio called pi. Nobody can dispute this, even non-scientists. We all have faith that this is the absolute truth in matters of areas of circles. However, why is pi precisely equal to 22 divided by 7? Why is it not 23 divided by 7, for example? This is something that cannot be explained by human logic.

If we turn to scripture, some things in the Bible defy human logic. For example, in the book of Genesis, we learn that Methuselah, the son of Enoch, father of Lamech, and grandfather of Noah, lived for 950 years (Genesis 5: 21-25). How is this possible? This is difficult to comprehend based on our limited human knowledge.

There are unfortunate instances in human history where differences in science and scripture have resulted in terrible disputes, some resulting in death. One of the worst examples of this phenomenon was the trial and execution of Giordano Bruno. He was executed by burning at the stake for advancing views considered heretical to Catholic doctrines. In 2000, the Vatican expressed regret for this atrocious act of violence in the name of advancing Biblical truth.[145]

The world is highly complex, and no amount of human reasoning can give us complete answers in our quest for the true meaning of life. We must make a leap of faith to understand the "un-understandable" in our physical world and the sacred texts.

Part Three

The Hard Questions

Chapter 7

Asking the Hard Questions

*"Courage doesn't happen when you have
all the answers. It happens when you are
ready to face the questions you have
been avoiding your whole life."*
—Shannon L. Alder

IN THE QUEST TO FIND the truth, it is essential to ask the right questions. Some of the most significant accomplishments in many spheres of life have emerged from asking questions and rigorously searching for answers. Indeed, the starting point for a research endeavor in many fields is finding a suitable research question. This is often the most important and, occasionally, the most challenging part of a research project. The French philosopher Jacques Voltaire once said: "Judge a man by his questions rather than by his answers."[146] No question should be out of bounds. This view is self-evident in scientific research but not to the same degree in other fields, such as politics and religion.

The "Why Question"

One of the best questions one could ask in any situation is, "Why?" Why do birds of a feather flock together? Why do the colors yellow and blue become green when mixed? Why are there only three primary colors (red, green, and blue) in the first place? Why did Christianity and Islam start in the Middle East and not East Asia?   Why is the sky blue? Why is the gestation period for human beings nine months while that of elephants is 22 months? Why do dogs bark while cows moo?

Finding answers to" why" questions can be interesting. If pursued with appropriate rigor, they can yield significant insights that apply to many aspects of life.

Here is a simplistic example from a business setting. In this instance, we will pursue the "Why?" question in several steps:

Salesman: Our sales for this month are 10% below last year.
Manager: Why?
Salesman: Because of stock issues in territory A.
Manager: Why?
Salesman: Our distributor Z failed to make deliveries to retailers in that territory on two consecutive days.
Manager: Why?
Salesman: One of the trucks was involved in an accident and was grounded for two days.

This simple illustration shows us that sales for a particular product dropped because of a logistics issue.

Engaging the distributor can help us find a quick and effective solution to the problem. In a business setting, asking "Why" questions can be invaluable for unlocking value.

According to research by two Harvard Business School professors (Weksler, Benny, 2016), asking questions:

..spurs learning and the exchange of ideas, it fuels innovation and performance improvement, it builds rapport and trust among team members. And it can mitigate business risk by uncovering unforeseen pitfalls and hazards.[147]

Below is another example from a different life domain.

Parent: Why did you come home late last night?
Son: Because I did not catch the 8:00 pm bus.
Parent: Why?
Son: Because I left school a little late.
Parent: Why?
Son: Because the teacher asked me to see him after class.
Parent: Why?
Son: Because I had not completed my homework.
Parent: Why had you not completed your homework?
Son: Because of the power blackout on Monday evening.

The parent in this scenario gains valuable insights into the reasons for his son's lateness from school. Therefore, they may invest in a simple solar power backup system to provide light at home during a power blackout.

Below is a third example, but it involves asking mental questions to obtain valuable personal insights.

Self: Why do I follow a particular religious faith?
Self: Because I believe it is the true religion.
Self: Why?
Self: Because that is what my parents told me.
Self: Why?
Self: Because that is what their forefathers taught them.

In this particular example, the question is a personal one seeking to find the source of our beliefs. In this specific instance, the endpoint is personal religious beliefs founded on the teachings of the missionaries who came to the country several decades ago.

◆◆◆

It is important to emphasize that the following inquiry is not intended to challenge the respective religions but to seek the truth and enhance our understanding.

We could also argue that we limit our understanding of religion by failing to ask questions. We would end up living a life premised on incorrect information. In certain situations, ignorance could lead to wrong decisions, sometimes with adverse consequences, even in matters of faith. An example of this is the case of Guidanno Bruno, mentioned in the preceding chapter, who was convicted by the Catholic church for heresy.

During his seven-year trial in Rome, he was held in confinement, sentenced to death, and burnt at the stake on 17 February 1600. His crime: Advancing the view that the earth was not the center of the universe, an idea contradictory to religious beliefs at the time.

The church's stance was later proved incorrect. The Vatican issued a posthumous apology to Guidanno Bruno 400 years later.[148,149]

There is another crucial point. Perhaps many non-believers do not belong to a particular faith simply because they have not been adequately exposed to religion. The questions we pose here and the answers we will find should hopefully benefit such people.

If we do not confront the difficult questions and seek answers, others may fill the vacuum with misleading explanations.

Failing to ask questions risks creating a negative dynamic similar to suppressing different opinions. To quote John Stuart Mill:

> *But the peculiar evil of silencing the expression of an opinion is that it is robbing the human race; posterity as well as the existing generation; those who dissent from the opinion, still more than those who hold it. If the opinion is right, they are deprived of the opportunity of exchanging error for truth: if wrong, they lose what is almost as great a benefit, the clearer perception and livelier impression of truth, produced by its collision with error. ... We can never be sure that the opinion we are endeavoring to stifle is a false opinion; and if we were sure, stifling it would be an evil still.[150]*

Finally, what is there to fear if we genuinely believe in our respective religions? In any event, the sacred texts we believe in should be unshakeable.

The Biggest Question of All

Most religions believe in the existence of a supernatural God. Why is there no concrete evidence of God other than what is written in the sacred texts of the various religions?

Questions Related to the Bible

When one reads the Bible, several "Why" questions emerge that are worth pondering. Scholars of theology may have ready answers to all of these questions. Still, posing them as part of our spiritual discovery and enlightenment journey is helpful.

Selected Questions by Donald Morgan

Writing in the SecularWeb, Morgan (2020) raises several pertinent questions regarding flaws, absurdities, inconsistencies, contradictions, questionable guidelines, and vulgarities and obscenities in the Bible. We will look at a few of the questions.[151]

In Luke Chapter 1, verses 26–38, the Bible describes how the angel Gabriel appeared before Mary and foretold her about the birth of Jesus. The angel told Mary that Jesus would rule over the house of Jacob forever, in a Kingdom with no end. Why has the latter part of this promise yet to be fulfilled?

Mathew Chapter 16, verse 28, says that Jesus told those listening to him that he would return before they died. Yet, everyone in question died before Jesus's return to earth. Why?

In the book of Mark, Chapter 16, verses 17 and 18, it is reported that Jesus told his disciples that if they believed in him, even handling snakes or drinking poison would not hurt them. Why would Jesus make such an assertion, yet some believers who tried to handle snakes and drink poison suffered harm?

In the book of Genesis, verse 1, it is stated that God created the earth. The question is, where did God dwell before the creation of the universe?

Genesis, Chapters 1 and 2 describe how God created Adam and Eve and the prohibitions he issued to Adam. Why did God not create a separation between Adam and the Tree of Eternal Life to prevent Adam and Eve from eating the fruit from the tree? Also, why did God let the serpent deceive Eve into eating fruit from the Tree of Eternal Life? And how was the snake able to communicate with Eve?

In Genesis Chapter 6, verse 4, the Bible states that giants on the earth came into contact with other humans and gave birth to other huge people. However, there is no historical evidence that supports the existence of giants. Why?

Genesis Chapter 32, verses 24-30, talks about a wrestling match between God and Jacob, in which Jacobs's hip is injured. Why would an all-powerful and all-merciful God engage in such a wrestling match?

In the Book of Genesis, Chapter 2, verse 17, it is stated that Adam would die on the day immediately after eating the forbidden fruit. In Chapter 5, verse 5, it is said that Adam lived for 930 years. Why is there such inconsistency?

In Proverbs chapter 15, verse 3, it is said that God sees everywhere. Why would God ask Cain about Abel's whereabouts, as stated in Genesis Chapter 4, verse 9?

The Bible says that God is loving and kind (Corinthians 13:11 and John 4:16). On the other hand, there are numerous sections where God is portrayed as angry, jealous, and vengeful. Sometimes, God is described as one who condones death and destruction (Genesis 4:15, Deuteronomy 32:19-27, Exodus 20:5; Joshua 10:30; Judges 14:19, and Ezekiel 9:5-7). Why is there such a contradiction in the Bible?

In Exodus 3:20-22, God instructs the Israelites to plunder Egypt, yet in Exodus 20:15, God says, "Thou shalt not steal." Why is there such inconsistency?

In Exodus 20:40, God says that people should not make statues, paintings, or any other type of image of anything. Why would God give such a guideline?

Exodus 31:15-17 states that no work should be done on Sabbath day. Infringement of this guideline is punishable by death. Why would God prescribe such a harsh punishment for the simple infraction of working on the seventh day of the week?

Deuteronomy 22:13-21 states that if a man marries a woman and discovers she is not a virgin, she should be stoned to death. Why would God prescribe such extraordinarily harsh punishment for such an infraction?

Mathew 5: 29-30 states that "...if thy right eye offend thee, pluck it out..." and "......if thy right hand offend thee, cut it off...". These guidelines seem pretty unusual. Why would God issue such guidelines?

In Genesis 19: 4-8, a story is narrated of a group of men baying for the blood of two male visitors of Lot. The men demand that Lot release the visitors so that the depraved men can have carnal knowledge with them. Lot offers his two daughters to the men instead. Why would the Bible contain a story of such vulgarity?

Genesis 19:30-38 describes how Lot, while drunk, engaged in amorous congress with his two daughters. Why would the Holy Bible contain such depictions of vulgarity?

Deuteronomy 21:10-14 states that when Israelites go to war, they should kidnap the beautiful women of their enemies. The Israelites should make the women their wives, and if the women fail to delight the men, the men should release the women. This information seems odd and vulgar. Why would the Bible contain such vulgarity?

Deuteronomy 23:1 says, "He that is wounded in the stones, or hath his privy member cut off, shall not enter into the congregation of the Lord." Why such vulgarity?

Several other questionable guidelines are found in the Bible, particularly in Genesis, Exodus, and Leviticus. Many other examples can be found in the books of Numbers, Deuteronomy, and Matthew.

The question that emerges from these and numerous other vulgarities listed by Morgan is why the Holy Bible would contain such information.

We shall explore possible answers to these questions in the next chapter.

Questions Related to Sacred Muslim Texts

Our purpose here is not to challenge Muslim religious texts. The idea is to share different perspectives from Muslim scholars to deepen our understanding of these sacred texts, as we have done with the Bible in the preceding section.

Questions Related to the Quran

If the words in the Quran are the words spoken by God, as is believed by followers of Islam, why is it that in some verses, Allah is speaking, while in others, Allah is not? Examples include Surah XVI. 81, XXVII. 61, xxxi. 9 and xliii. 10.[152,153]

Perhaps the most controversial *surahs* in the Quran are *Surah an-Najm* (Star) 53:19-22 and *Surah Hajj* (Pilgrimage) 22:52-53, known as the "Story of the Cranes." It is claimed that the verses in *Surah* 53:19-22 regarding the deities *al-Lat*, *al-Uzza*, and *Manat* were communicated to Muhammad by Satan through deception. The angel Gabriel subsequently informed Muhammad that the deities were idols, necessitating the correction recorded in *Surah* 22:52-53. Some scholars have claimed that this is inconsistent with the assertion that the verses in the Quran are the words of God that are unchangeable.[154]

In his highly controversial book *"Why I am not Muslim,"* Warraq (2003) asks multiple questions. For example, he asks why God cannot control his subjects and why he is angry and jealous if he is omnipotent, omniscient, and benevolent.

Above all, why did God select an Arabian merchant as his messenger? Ibn Warraq argues that these actions do not seem consistent with those of a Supreme Being. Why?[155]

According to John Wansbrough, Patricia Crone, and Yehuda D. Nevo, the available historical evidence shows that the Quran was written many years after Muhammad's death.[156] The Quran is believed to consolidate the verbal accounts of people close to Prophet Muhammad. Some of these accounts may not have been accurate verbatim accounts of what Muhammad said. Why, then, do Muslims believe that the words in the Quran were spoken directly by God?

There is a follow-up question relating to the claim that God's words in the Quran were spoken directly by God. The first *surah* (*Al-Fatiha*) is a prayer to God. There are other examples (*surah* 114, 17.1, 27.91, 19.64, 37.161, and 166). So, why is there such a fundamental inconsistency in the attribution of the words in the Quran?[157]

Initially, there were several versions of the Quran. They included codices by Ibn Masud, Ubai b, Kab, Ali', Abu Bakr, al-Ash'ari, al-Aswad, and others. Uthman then mandated that Muslims should adhere to his codex. The Uthman version became the definitive codex. The other versions were destroyed.[158] So, if the Quran contains unchangeable words spoken directly by God, as Muslims believe, then why were there different versions of the texts at the time of Uthman?

Other verses repudiate several verses in the Quran.[159] Some estimates run to 500 such repudiations, leading Dashti to ask:

> *Is it fitting that an All-Powerful, Omniscient, and Omnipotent God should revise His commands so many times? Does He need to issue commands that .... need revising so often? Why can He not get it right the First time? After all, He is all-wise. Why does He not reveal the better verse first?[160]*

Various scholars have pointed to questionable guidelines in the Quran. *Surah* 4.13, for example, states that men should discipline their women by striking them if the women are disobedient. There have been debates about the interpretation of this *surah*. Still, some see it as a questionable guideline from the holy Quran. They ask: why would God issue an instruction that appears so demeaning to women?

Surah 9:29 of the Quran says Muslims should go to war with unbelievers. It reads as follows:

> *Fight those who do not believe in Allah or in the Last Day and who do not consider unlawful what Allah and His Messenger have made unlawful and who do not adopt the religion of truth from those who were given the Scripture - [fight] until they give the jizyah willingly while they are humbled.*

Why would the supreme God instruct people to go to war, particularly war directed at unbelievers?

Some commentators have noted that *surahs* 4:24, 2:223, and 111 contain obscenities. However, there is an unsettled debate about that perspective, as the *surahs* do not seem as explicit as alleged.

Questions Related to the Hadith and Sunnah

Muslim scholars and theologians have extensively debated the authenticity of the Hadith and Sunnah. Today, Muslim denominations are based on differing interpretations of the Hadith and Sunnah. However, there is unanimity amongst all Muslims that the Quran is the primary sacred text.

Some Muslims, such as the scholar Rashad Khalifa, believe that Muhammad forbade references to teachings other than the Quran.[161]

Others take a more liberal view and follow some Hadith and Sunnah texts. For example, Sunni Muslims follow the Hadith collection called *Qutub al-Sittah*, compiled by Abu Hurairah. The texts include the six main books (*Sahih Sittah*) of Hadith: *Sahi al-Bukhari, Sahi Muslim, Sunan as-Sughra, Sunan Abu Dawood, Jami al-Tirmidhi*, and *Sunan ibn Majah*.

The Shia Muslims, on the other hand, follow the *Kutub al-Arba'a hadith*, comprised of four principle books, namely, *Kitab al-Kafi* compiled by Muhammad ibn Ya'qub al-Kulayni al-Razi; *Man La Yahduruhu al-Faqih* compiled by Muhammad ibn Babawayh, and *Tahdhib al-Ahkam* and *Al-Istibsar*, both of which were compiled by Shaykh Muhammad Tusi.

◆◆◆

With this context in mind, we will briefly examine some of the questions that emerge from reviewing the Hadith and Sunnah.

The various collections of the narrations (*hadith*) of the actions and sayings (*sunnah*) of Prophet Muhammad were compiled by his followers several generations after his death. Therefore, the authenticity of some of the hadith has come into question. For example, Rashad Khalifa claims that some narratives are fabrications.[162] Some theologians and scholars have also averred that the accuracy of some of the hadith texts is suspect. These theologians and scholars believe that some players doctored some narratives to accomplish political or sectarian interests.[163]

There are multiple inconsistencies and contradictions in the Hadith. Below are some examples.[164]

Wudhu is the Muslim ritual for cleansing parts of the body. The Hadith narration by Ibn Abbas states that it should be done only once a day. On the other hand, the narration by Abdullah bin Zaid states that it should be done twice.

The *hadith* narrated by Anas bin Malik says that when Muhammad was 40, Allah sent him to Mecca and stayed there for ten years. On the other hand, the *hadith* by Ibn Abbas talks of 13 years.

According to *Surah* 24.2 of the Quran, the punishment for adultery is 100 lashes. Then, in Book 29, Number 19 of Hadith, Ubada b. as-Samit added that the punishment for adultery in the case of a married woman is stoning to death.

Some guidelines in the Hadith are questionable. For example, Sahih Bukhari Hadith Book 67, Number 127, narrated by Abu Huraira, reads as follows:

The Prophet said, "If a man invites his wife to sleep with him and she refuses to come to him, then the angels send their curses on her till morning.[165]

Sahih Bukhari Hadith Book 77, Number 165, narrated by Abu Talha, reads as follows:

The Prophet said, "Angels do not enter a house which has either a dog or a picture in it.[166]

Sahih Bukhari Hadith Book 59, Number 83, narrated by Abu Said Al-Khudri, reads as follows:

The Prophet said, "If while you are praying, somebody intends to pass in front of you, prevent him; and should he insist, prevent him again; and if he insists again, fight with him (i.e., prevent him violently, e.g., pushing him violently), because such a person is (like) a devil.[167]

Various scholars have also raised their eyebrows regarding the obscenities and vulgarities in the Hadith and Sunnah. Below are a few examples.

Bukhari Hadith 5068 Book 67, Hadith 6, narrated by Anas, reads as follows:

The Prophet used to go round (have sexual relations with) all his wives in one night, and he had nine wives.[168]

Bukhari Hadith 268 Book 5, Hadith 21, narrated by Qatada, states that:

Anas bin Malik said, "The Prophet used to visit all his wives in a round, during the day and night and they were eleven in number." I asked Anas, "Had the Prophet the strength for it?" Anas replied, "We used to say that the Prophet was given the strength of thirty (men)." And Sa`id said on the authority of Qatada that Anas had told him about nine wives only (not eleven).[169]

Sahih Bukhari Hadith Book 59, Number 74, narrated by Ibn 'Umar, reads as follows:

The Prophet said, "Fever is from the heat of the (Hell) Fire; so abate fever with water.[170]

Sahih Bukhari Hadith Book 67, Number 31, narrated by Abdullah bin Umar, reads as follows:

Allah's Messenger said, "Evil omen is in the women, the house and the horse."[171]

Questions Related to Sacred Hindu Texts

Although Hindus use numerous religious texts, our inquiry will focus on only two significant texts: the Vedas and the Bhagavad Gita.

Questions Related to the Vedas

According to Narendra Nath:

Vedas could not have come into existence before human beings appeared on this earth and before the Sanskrit language came into existence. And there are no good reasons for believing that the Sanskrit language came into existence even before human beings appeared on this earth![172]

The Vedas contain traces of the old Vedic religions, which worshiped different types of spirits that dwelt in stones, animals, trees, rivers, mountains, and stars. An example is the Atharva Veda, which contains spells intended to destroy enemies, woo sleep, etc. [173]

Narendra Nath states that:

A Brahmin, according to Manu [Manusmriti], must not teach the Shudra and woman even if he dies with his knowledge without imparting it to anybody. [73] On the other hand, if anyone studies the Vedas on his own, he or she will go straight to hell.[174]

The Vedas contain creation stories that are inconsistent with each other. For example, one God may be described as the greatest, but another God later in the text is also described as the greatest.[175]

There are six systems of Hindu thought: *Mimamsa, Vedanta, Sankhya, Yoga, Nyaya*, and *Vaisheshika*. The Nyaya believe that the Vedas are God's word. Yet, the Hindu belief system is generally premised on the existence of many gods.

The Mimansa are an exception; they do not believe in gods, yet they believe that the Vedas are eternal and are not the work of any humankind.[176]

The caste system (*Varna-vyavastha*), described in the Purusha–Sukta of the Rig Veda, seems inherently discriminatory. Discrimination appears in other Hindu texts in different forms, too. For example, the Ramayana states that Ram killed Shambuka, a Shudra by birth, just because Shambuka was doing rigorous exercises. A person of his caste was not supposed to do such exercises.

Another example is in the Mahabharata. We learn that Dronacharya refused to teach Eklavya archery because Eklavya was not born a Kshatriya. When Dronacharya learned that Eklavya had taught himself archery, he forced him to cut a piece of his right thumb. Cutting his thumb ensured he could not become better than Arjuna, another archery student from the Kshatriya caste. [177]

The caste system goes beyond the allocation of duties. It applies to the meting out of punishment for crimes and even payment of interest on loans, with the lower castes being at a relative disadvantage to the higher castes.[178]

The caste system is also against freedom of choice of occupation, residence, and selection of a marriage partner.[179] Narendra Nath states that:

Manusmriti is full of abusive epithets for freethinkers and non-believers. The unorthodox (nastikas) is sometimes equated with the Shudras, sometimes with the Chandalas, sometimes with thieves and sometimes with lunatics! [79] Such is the generosity of Hindu dharma.[180]

Rig Veda 10.110.5, Atharva Veda 14.2.38, Yajur Veda 19.88, and Yajur Veda 23.19-21 contain obscenities, but perhaps sex was not associated with vulgarity when the Vedas were written.

Questions Related to the Bhagavad Gita

Many Hindus consider the Bhagavad Gita one of the most important sacred texts. It is an extension of the epic story, Mahabharata. However, in this instance, the Bhagavad Gita is a story involving Krishna and Arjuna. Arjuna is an archer, while Krishna, a preacher, is his charioteer. They are in a war situation, and Arjuna suddenly realizes that he is on the verge of killing several members of his family and relatives. He engages Krishna in a philosophical dialogue on how to conduct himself in these circumstances. The conversation extends over 700 verses. Krishna gives Arjuna immensely insightful life lessons covering a broad scope of subjects, from the meaning of life to the ideal diet for a fulfilling life.

Although the Bhagavad Gita is one of the cornerstones of the Hindu religion, some believers do not consider it a strictly sacred text but a helpful guidebook on how best to lead one's life. However, other believers maintain that it contains the word of God. Our review of its contents below should be interpreted in this dichotomous context.

The conversation between Krishna and Arjuna narrated in the Bhagavad Gita was exceptionally long. It seems odd that the combatants in the war described in the Mahabharata could have waited so long for Krishna and Arjuna to finish the conversation before the war could start.[181]

Some critics of the Gita also point out that Krishna once told Arjuna that action was the most important thing. A little later, Krishna states that knowledge is the most important thing.[182]

The Gita also presents Krishna as God and a superhuman. This double meaning makes interpreting some parts of the text challenging.[183]

Another challenge relates to the inter-relationship between *dharma* and *karma*. In other words, as Arjuna engages in the war, his skill could be interpreted as a manifestation of his *dharma*. It could also be related to *karma* and, therefore, entirely independent of his ability. This matter is somewhat confusing.[184]

The Bhagavad Gita supports the discriminative caste system (*Varna-vyavastha*), as evidenced by the two verses below.

Ch.4, Verse 13: Krishna:
"The four-fold caste system has been created by Me according to the differentiation of Guna and Karma;"

Ch.18, verse.41: Krishna:
"Of Brahmanas, Kshatriyas, and Vaishyas, as also the Sudras, O Arjuna, the duties are distributed according to the qualities born of their own nature."

The Gita has also been criticized for violating the principle of non-violence (*Ahimsa)* in ancient Hindu religious texts. For example, Krishna urges Arjuna to fight on. Yet, Krishna is aware that members of Arjuna's family are likely to die in the process.

Unlike other religious texts, the Gita does not appear to have any vulgarities or obscenities.

Questions Related to the Buddhist Tipitaka

Buddhists do not believe in a supreme figurehead. Their faith is based on several rules and practices codified in the Tipitaka. One could conjecture that Buddhism would not exist as we know it today if it were not for this text. Accordingly, as we have done with the sacred texts of other religions, it would be interesting to find out whether the Tipitaka raises any pertinent questions.

◆◆◆

Some commentators have pointed out that the Tipitaka discriminates against women. The discrimination is because the book contains more rules for nuns than monks.

However, it is also noteworthy that Gautama Buddha explicitly stated that his desire was for the equitable treatment of women (Amida Buddha's vow 35).[185]

◆◆◆

The conduct of some Buddhists, which one would imagine is shaped by the rules of behavior prescribed by the Tipitaka, raises several questions. For example, Buddhist monks have been accused of involvement in politics, especially in Sri Lanka.

The words of Maduluwawe Sobhita, while addressing the Buddhist *sangha* council at the Visuddharamaya temple in Colombo in March 1983, speak for themselves:

Some say that monks do not need politics, but we cannot do anything except through politics. Even if we do not endorse party politics, we have to take certain decisions in important situations. We should have the right to comment on good and bad things that the government does...[I]f a government engages in things that are against the religion (Buddhism) and the nation, it becomes necessary for Buddhist monks to appoint a new government.[186]

Also, there are several sections of the Tikitaka where violence is forbidden, notably the Kakacūpama Sutta, Majjhima-Nikāya 28 at MN i 128-29, which states that:

Bhikkhus, even if bandits were to sever you savagely limb by limb with a two-handled saw, he who gave rise to a mind of hate towards them would not be carrying out my teaching.

However, as pointed out by Michael Jerryson and Mark Juergensmeyer, there are instances in history where Buddhist leaders have sanctioned violence and war.[187]

Final Questions on All Religious Texts

The last two questions are: Why are there so many religions and religious texts? Secondly, if a God existed, why would he reveal himself in so many different ways in different parts of the world?

Chapter 8

Answers from Philosophy

"The unexamined life is not worth living."
– Socrates

THE QUESTIONS RAISED IN THE previous chapter are difficult to answer. However, as we continue to seek enlightenment, we will not try to answer every question. That would be a herculean task that professional theologians should best undertake. Instead, we will try to seek understanding from a holistic perspective. To this end, we will start by looking at how philosophers have attempted to answer the big questions. In other words, how philosophers have tried to explain using logical reasoning.

It is also important to state that one can live an entirely fulfilling and happy life without necessarily finding clear-cut philosophical answers to all the difficult questions relating to religion. The plain truth is that some of the questions cannot be answered rationally despite the excellent attempts by philosophers over the years.[188]

The philosophical inquiry will help validate the underlying premises of one's beliefs. And if the questions remain unanswered, one will at least come out of it wiser and with a significantly better understanding of life.

What is Philosophy?

But let us first reflect on the meaning of philosophy. Different scholars have defined philosophy differently. For our purposes, we will stick with the following definition from the Oxford Desk Dictionary, namely, that philosophy is:

> *1 use of reason and argument to seek knowledge of the causes and nature of things and the principles governing existence 2a particular system or set of or set of beliefs reached by this b personal rule of life.*[189]

Interestingly, until the 1600s, philosophy encompassed multiple subject areas, including the sciences. Sciences such as physics and chemistry were called "natural philosophy." However, later, a clear distinction was made between philosophy and other fields of study.[190]

The main idea here is to look for answers to the questions posed in the preceding chapter holistically, using logical reasoning or in an intuitively plausible manner.

Philosophy of Religion

The Internet Encyclopedia of Philosophy defines the philosophy of religion as follows:

> *Philosophy of religion is the philosophical study of the meaning and nature of religion. It includes the analyses of religious concepts, beliefs, terms, arguments, and practices of religious adherents.*[191]

The scope of the philosophy of religion is extensive. We will only scratch the surface, but this should suffice. Accordingly, we will follow the path of the philosophy of religion charted out by Meister (2020), the author of the *Philosophy of Religion* section in the *Encyclopedia of Philosophy*.[192]

According to Meister, the philosophy of religion tries to address the big questions of religion under six major themes: religious language and belief, religious diversity, concepts of God / Ultimate Reality, arguments for and against the existence of God, problems of evil and suffering, and miracles. We will explore the big questions of religion using this philosophical framework.[193]

If you are a non-philosopher, then please be warned! Indulging in matters of philosophy can sometimes yield unexpected results. Just remember the following philosophy story as you go through the rest of this chapter:

A philosopher tells a friend she's recently had a baby. The friend says, "Congratulations. Is it a boy or a girl?" The philosopher says, "Yes."[194]

If, at this point, you are feeling a little jingoistic about philosophy and want to practice more on what to expect, read the first chapter of Martin Heidegger's *Being and Time*.[195] You can find a free *e-book* version of it on the internet. And if you start feeling a little dizzy in the middle of that chapter, do not say you were not cautioned.

But at least there is one guarantee. After reading *Being and Time*, you will fully appreciate why the book is available on the internet free of charge.

Language and Belief

The language used in religion is sometimes couched in mysterious or vague language. Because of this, some philosophers, called logical positivists, hold that religious beliefs based on such language cannot be empirically confirmed. According to them, such ideas are meaningless.

However, in recent years, starting in the mid-1880s, philosophers such as Ludwig Wittgenstein (1889–1951) have demonstrated that such logical positivist views are shortsighted. According to Wittgenstein, one must go beyond what can be empirically or scientifically tested and examine the underlying meaning of the language used in sacred religious texts.[196]

However, even among the non-empiricists, there are two camps: realists and non-realists.[197]

The realists aver that even if one cannot find physical evidence to support many core religious beliefs, the mere fact that such beliefs exist is a manifestation of the veracity of the underlying religious concepts. Further, religion is about faith and trust—nothing more.

The non-realists, on the other hand, believe that ideas about the existence of physical evidence to support religious claims of things that exist in a supernatural realm are irrelevant. They contend that religion is a human construct that serves a particular purpose in human beings' lives. Further, religious claims are made within a certain social context and should only be interpreted within that context.

There are different shades of arguments made by realists and non-realists to support their points of view. However, like most matters of philosophy, there has yet to be a consensus.

John Mucai

Religious Diversity

Turning to religious diversity, there is a growing appreciation of the diversity in religious beliefs and practices. Some religions have a few overlaps and divergencies in beliefs. For example, Christians and Muslims believe in one God, while Hindus believe in multiple gods. On the other hand, Buddhists do not believe in a supreme figurehead.[198]

There are three distinct schools of thought on the question of religious diversity. The first school, the religious pluralists, led by Hick (1990), believes there is only one Ultimate Reality. Further, Ultimate Reality is perceived differently by adherents of different religions, like the parable of the elephant and the blind men. In other words, all religions share different experiences of the same phenomenon and tailor their spiritual and linguistic practices accordingly. [199]

One criticism of this perspective is that it suggests that all religions have a partial picture. Additionally, only an amalgamation of all religions would allow the revelation of the complete Ultimate Reality—something that would only be possible with the formation of one syncretistic religion.

The second school of thought is religious relativism, with Joseph Runzo as one of its key proponents. The basic idea behind religious relativism is that religious truth is relative. In other words, one's truth claims regarding the Ultimate Truth depend on one's cultural background and the worldview of the community where one comes from.

This school of thought is very similar to the pluralist school, except for one difference. The pluralists subscribe to one universal Ultimate Reality. In contrast, relativists believe truth is relative, depending on one's background.[200]

According to Meister (2009), most adherents of world religions belong to the third school of religious exclusivism. People in this school hold that the central tenets of their faith are the correct ones and that the beliefs of other religions are false. In other words, salvation can only be found exclusively in their religion. This view has been the source of many intractable differences between religions and generated religious intolerance in different parts of the world. Some people consider the exclusivist school as arrogant, dishonest, and oppressive. Further, epistemologically, it is a perspective not founded on justifiable truth claims.[201]

Concepts of God and Ultimate Reality

Ultimate Reality

Concepts of God and Ultimate Reality are the core of religious beliefs worldwide. Different religions hold primarily two views.[202]

Firstly, the monothetic belief is held by Western religions: Christianity, Islam, and Judaism. These religions hold that there is only one God—an all-powerful, personal God who created and sustains the heavens and the earth, a God who knows everything, has unlimited power, and is unchangeable.

On the other hand, Eastern religions such as Hinduism perceive Ultimate Reality as the absolute state of being.

The two differing perspectives of God and Ultimate Reality result in differing views on life and death and the actions that followers of the religion believe they need to take to achieve salvation.

The Existence of God

Three philosophical arguments—ontological, cosmological, and teleological—are generally used to explain God's existence.[203]

The Ontological Argument

The ontological argument was first propounded by Saint Anselm of Canterbury (1033–1109). The argument states that the most perfect being we can imagine must be God. Because we cannot conceive of a higher being, that great being must exist not only in the imagination but also in reality.

The Cosmological Argument

The cosmological argument has three variants: the Thomistic contingency argument, the Leibnizian sufficient reason argument, and the Kalam argument.

The Thomistic contingency argument is attributable to Thomas Aquinas (1225–1274). It holds that the universe owes its existence to something else and that that something else is God.

The Leibnizan sufficient reason argument is attributable to Gottfried Wilhelm Leibniz (1646–1716). It holds that there must be a sufficient reason for the universe's existence and that the explanation of that existence must be a supreme God.

The Kalam (speculative theology) argument comes from Islam and goes as follows:

1. *Everything that begins to exist has a cause of its existence.*
2. *The universe began to exist.*
3. *Therefore, the universe has a cause of its existence.*
4. *Since no scientific explanation (in terms of physical laws) can provide a causal account of the origin (very beginning) of the universe, the cause must be personal (explanation is given in terms of a personal agent).*[204,205]

The proponents of the Kalam argument hold that even the "Big Bang" phenomenon that some scientists say gave rise to the universe is attributable to "a non-temporal, non-spatial, personal, transcendent cause—namely God."[206]

Teleological argument

The core of the teleological argument is that the nature of the universe suggests the existence of an intelligent, purposeful grand design and that the designer must be God. One of the strongest proponents of this perspective was William Paley (1743–1805).

There are numerous other variations of the teleological argument. For example, the fine-tuning arguments suggest that nature is so fine-tuned in terms of nuclear forces and gravity that the fine-tuning could only be attributable to God. Other perspectives point to complex systems such as DNA and consciousness, which could not have emerged just from anywhere other than through the actions of a supreme being, namely, God.

◆◆◆

A key point to note is that all these arguments point to the existence of a supernatural being called God, but not a specific God for Christians, Muslims, Hindus, or any other religion.

◆◆◆

Others have also adduced various arguments for the non-existence of God. For example, some point out that none of the arguments for the existence of God is indubitable. Others have argued that certain claims are inconsistent with scientific proof.

Another argument is that the various claims regarding God's existence do not explain why there is so much suffering and pain.

◆◆◆

Advances in science and technology have challenged religion. However, the voices of opposition are gradually drowned out as respect for belief in God re-emerges, even within the scientific community.

◆◆◆

Various arguments within the philosophical community have also been opposed to the veracity of claims about God's different attributes, such as omniscience and omnipotence. However, as Søren Kierkegaard (1813–1855) pointed out, religion does not require rational justification; it is a matter of faith.

Problems of Evil and Suffering

Now, we turn to the problems of evil and suffering in the world. Philosophers have debated much about reconciling the idea of an all-powerful and all-loving God with the reality of evil and suffering.[207]

This apparent contradiction has been used to dismiss the existence of God. However, this argument has been refuted because it assumes that an all-powerful and all-loving God would wish for a world free of evil and suffering. It is quite feasible that evil and suffering exist to teach humankind, on whom God bestowed free will, the virtues of good morality (including compassion and mercy).[208]

Another point that has been the subject of debate relates to God's hiddenness. If God is all-loving and all-powerful, why does He not reveal Himself so that even those who do not believe in His existence can see and feel Him and refrain from sinful acts? Various arguments have been given to counter this perspective. This is still an open issue, even among theologians.[209]

Religions that believe in reincarnation and karma have presented the view that acts of evil are punished in the afterlife. Such punishment may seem to cause much unwarranted suffering. However, suffering could represent restitution for one's evil deeds in a previous life. Using this logic, one could argue that when someone suffers for sins committed in an earlier life, it follows that the one causing the suffering in the current life is performing a necessary act sanctioned by God. This view does not seem fair. Once again, the solution to evil and suffering offered by karma and reincarnation arguments is incomplete.[210]

Miracles

The final point from the philosophy of religion relates to miracles. Theologians and philosophers have debated the subject of miracles extensively.[211] One view holds that there is no concrete evidence to support the notions of the phenomenon that defy the laws of nature described in religious texts or oral religious literature. On the other hand, the critics point out that supernatural phenomena can be legitimately attributed to an all-powerful God who is, in any event, the creator of everything that happens in the world, including what humankind perceives as the laws of nature.

Part Four

My Submissions

Chapter 9

My Submissions

"I would rather have questions that can't be answered than answers that can't be questioned."
—*Richard Feynman*

I HOPE YOU HAVE FOUND our journey up to this point enlightening. The most astounding revelation has been the sheer enormity of literature on different aspects of religion, from sacred religious texts to other scholarly works. Yet, all that information seems to point to the quest to find life's hidden meaning and the overwhelming desire to determine the personal and collective actions required to fulfill life's purpose.

Are there other answers to the many complex questions we explored in the previous chapters? Based on my insights from the journey thus far, I would submit that the answer is a resounding "Yes." But these answers are personal.

The Existence of God

To me, the evidence of God's existence is all around us. As I write this book and look out the window, I cannot help but marvel at the immense beauty in the world's various forms.

A few meters from where I am sitting, I can see a *Nandi flame* tree blossoming with red flowers. Three weeks ago, I looked out the window and did not see as many flowers. So, during the past few days, a miracle happened without my knowledge, just to reveal itself in immeasurable beauty this morning.

Even as I type these words, I can hear the beautiful chirping sounds of birds. I am not sure what the birds are saying, but they must surely be saying something to each other. Otherwise, they would just keep quiet. The loud and animated sounds suggest the birds must be happy or excited about something. Perhaps they are enjoying the freshness brought about by last night's torrential downpour.

In the background, I can hear the sound of water flowing in a nearby stream. The stream has been flowing nonstop since my family, and I moved into this neighborhood more than ten years ago. Where has all that water been coming from for all those years?

How about the two huge *travelers* palm trees slowly fanning their huge paddle-shaped leaves? These trees have been growing slowly for the last ten years, from small plants to tall majestic plants, creating an aesthetic beauty in the outdoors that is difficult to describe.

How about the blue sky? Two hours ago, the sky was completely clear. The sun was shining beautifully. I could not wait to adorn my sports shoes and go for a walk to enjoy the sunshine under the deep blue sky. But now, some white and grey clouds have appeared almost from nowhere. They are covering the sun. I am sure this is a momentary phenomenon. Later in the day, the clouds will continue on their journey and probably turn into raindrops that will go into the soil and provide nutrition to multiple plants.

I have just seen a butterfly. I only saw it for a few seconds. It is probably standing on a flower right now, looking for butterfly food. It will then fly onto other flowers until later in the day when it decides to rest, just as I will do.

A little further away, I can see an acacia tree hidden amongst several grevillea trees. The *acacia* tree looks unique compared to the other trees. I have been near it several times, and one of its key features is its thorny branches. Where did those thorns come from, and why do the *grevillea* trees not have similar thorns?

I can also see some banana plants near the house of one of my neighbors. The plants have remained the same since I started seeing them about two years ago. I can imagine that they have provided nourishment to my neighbor every nine months.

My wife, Susan, asked me to join her for tea in the living room a while ago. I drank the nice-tasting tea harvested from the beautiful, lush Limuru tea plantations, just a 40-minute drive from here. Just the thought of the Limuru tea plantations makes me feel good.

At 5:00 am this morning, I was woken up by heavy rain. Where did it come from? It was raining heavily. Water was everywhere, falling from the sky in multiple droplets, creating mini-streams outside the house. The water must have come from the clouds I watched from my window yesterday afternoon. And why did they fall in droplets? Why did the droplets not fall from the sky all at once?

The air outside was cool and fresh. How nice! The freshness was a lovely welcome to a brand-new day.

It struck me vividly that the grass outside the house would turn dark green in the next few days, thanks to the heavy rain.

The sky is now covered with grey clouds. Where did they all come from? The blue skies I watched a short while ago are all covered with grey clouds, except for a few patches on the extreme right-hand side of the window. At first glance, I thought the clouds were stationary, but now I can see some movement. They are moving very slowly in a southerly direction under the influence of an invisible force.

◆◆◆

We do indeed live in a wonderful world. I do not need any other evidence to convince me that nature's immeasurable beauty and complexity right before my eyes are attributable to God.

As described in the preceding chapters, this must be the work of the all-powerful Christian God, the Muslim God; Allah, the God of the Hindus; Brahma, the creator of everything; and Ngai, the God of the Kikuyus. Although Buddhists do not believe in a supreme figurehead, the teachings of Gautama Buddha describe a state of *nirvana* that is attained through a deep insight into the true nature of life. I submit that the state of *nirvana* is also attributable to God.

None of the religions we have covered in the preceding chapters is flawless based on human logic. But that does not negate the magnificence of the wonders right before our eyes.

Even atheists who do not follow a particular religion can hardly dispute the wonder and complexity of the world described above. To what would they attribute it?

Shortcomings in the Sacred Religious Texts

The one common feature of all sacred texts reviewed in the preceding chapters is that they were compilations of manuscripts written by several people. In many instances, the texts were based on oral accounts handed down from generation to generation over many years - sometimes even hundreds of years. Therefore, it is reasonable to conclude that some information may have become distorted during transmission.

Therefore, it is no wonder that some texts contain apparent flaws, absurdities, inconsistencies, contradictions, questionable guidelines, vulgarities, and obscenities. These shortcomings are simply manifestations of human limitations.

To cite John Barton, formerly professor of holy scriptures at the University of Oxford and the author *of A History of the Bible: The Books and Its Faiths*:

> *The Old Testament is not a work of fiction, but nor is it a modern piece of history-writing.*[212]

The same could apply to other religious texts.

The flaws, which comprise a small percentage of the sacred documents' contents, do not negate the basic idea of God's existence. Miraculously, the texts were handed down from generation to generation over centuries without losing their deep religious meaning to followers.

The Veracity of the Sacred Texts

What can be said about the integrity of the sacred texts? I will never know the answer to this question. That is because the information that we would need to test the integrity of the texts is contained within the texts themselves. For example, there are many instances where a text includes a claim made by a person, and that person is the only person who is privy to the source of that information. We do not have any other external evidence to corroborate the claim.

It seems that examining the texts to determine the integrity of their source would be littered with a minefield of unverifiable claims and counter-claims in equal measure.

But should it matter that there is no practical way of verifying the claims in the texts? No.

If the texts align with my conception of God, they are good enough for me, with or without defects. We are all endowed with the intellect to determine the contents of the holy writings that are inconsistent with the spirit of the entire document, and that should, therefore, be ignored.

Perhaps the right question to ask is whether the texts, in essence, prescribe a way of living that promotes harmony amongst members of the human race and the environment. Secondly, whether the texts provide reliable insights into the true meaning of life? Thirdly, do the texts contain consistent messages that are sustainable over time? If the answers to these questions are affirmative, then, to their adherents, the texts serve their purpose.

Further, whether or not one would consider the contents of some sacred texts fantastical or not, they were all written with the noblest of intentions. They were primarily aimed at making us well-rounded human beings, capable of co-existing in harmony with one another and nature – giving us hope amidst the myriad of challenges we encounter daily. Anything in the sacred texts that suggests anything to the contrary was most likely included unintentionally. Alternatively, it may have been included with the right intent but was couched in language that made it susceptible to misinterpretation.

The Different Religions

Why are there so many religions in the world? And why would God reveal Himself in different ways in different parts of the world?

There is a simple answer to these two questions. God manifests himself in his wonder and majesty in the same complex and unknowable way everywhere. This fact is evident in all religions. And over time, people in different parts of the world have chosen to worship God in their unique ways based on their evolving cultures and traditions.

Accordingly, everyone should be free to choose the religion that best suits their circumstances based on their respective cultural background, stations in life, and location.

Schism Between Religious Practices and Traditional Cultural Practices

The antagonism between religious practices and other cultural practices described previously is perhaps a microcosm of what could be happening in different shapes and forms in other parts of the world. At its core are the multiple and unique ways people put their religious beliefs into "practice" vis-à-vis other entrenched cultural practices. It does not seem to be a clash between religious "beliefs" about God.

Religion teaches tolerance, accommodation, and adherence to certain fundamental principles of common decency and morality. The same principles can be found in most cultures, too.

Accordingly, the various schisms between religious practices and other cultural practices are part of the phenomenon captured by the Kikuyu proverb that says that axes in one basket must hit against each other (*Mathanwa mari kiondo kimwe matiagaga gukomorania*).

Religion and Science

Some people have said that there is a divide between religious beliefs and science. I would submit that such views are misplaced. Science and religion are mutually inclusive in many respects.

The problem starts when people start dwelling on details. If you look at the details, then a lot of what is written in the religious texts is not supported by concrete scientific facts. A good example is the story of creation. According to science, the earth is millions of years old. Yet, most religions suggest that the earth was created a few thousand years ago. Scientists and religious people who hold dogmatic positions on such issues should turn inwards and seek inspiration on how they could find a point of intersection with those who have different views from them.

We need to remember, as stated previously, that most religious texts are narratives handed down over many years, from generation to generation. And the substance of what was in the original message could have been lost as the information was transmitted across generations. So, what was perhaps originally intended as a legend or myth could have trickled down the ages and ended up being incorrectly interpreted as fact.

Similarly, scientific theories grounded on excellent facts eventually hit a solid wall when subjected to the simple test of the successive "whys." For example, scientists will say that the world was formed 13.7 billion years ago through a "Big Bang" that occurred spontaneously.

But why did the "Big Bang" occur at that specific time? And why don't we hear of "Big Bangs" happening in other parts of the universe nowadays? I submit that no scientist can stand up and answer these questions with a straight face.

One of my favorite mathematical formulae is the Euler identity, a well-known formula in the scientific community. This formula never ceases to mesmerize me. It links five fundamental mathematical constants:

$$e^{i\pi} + 1 = 0$$

e – the number that underlies exponential growth
i – the "imaginary" square root of -1
$$\sqrt{4} = 2$$
$$\sqrt{-1} = i$$
π or pi – the ratio of the circumference of a circle to its diameter
1 – the basis of all other numbers
0 – the concept of nothingness

In a poll conducted by *The Mathematical Intelligencer* in 1990, readers of the journal voted this formula as the most beautiful mathematical formulae of all time.[213] The question that never ceases to baffle me is why this formula works so perfectly. Where did that remarkable symmetry come from?

There are many other scientific formulae with similarly astonishing characteristics.

I submit that the world would be better if scientists collaborated with the religious community in the never-ending search for true knowledge. Further, I submit that science and religion are two sides of the same coin.

Part Five

Faith in Action

Chapter 10

Living in Faith

*"Faith is taking the first step even when
you don't see the whole staircase."*
- Martin Luther King, Jr.

THIS CHAPTER IS A CALL for us to reflect on our faith in God. It starts by considering the meaning of faith and how this is linked to our perpetual quest for the true meaning of life. This is followed by a brief narration of the story of Abraham and Isaac, one of the best stories in the Bible regarding unshakeable faith in God.

◆◆◆

What is Faith?

Faith can be defined as "complete trust or confidence in someone or something" or "strong belief in the doctrines of a religion, based on spiritual conviction rather than proof."[214] Faith in God opens the door for the beginning of the journey towards understanding our purpose in this world.

The Story of Abraham and Isaac

The story of Abraham and Isaac is one of the fascinating stories in the Bible, demonstrating unshakeable faith in God. It is narrated in Genesis, the first book of the Bible.

In the first few chapters of Genesis (1–11), we learn about the creation of heaven and earth, the story of Adam and Eve, and how their rebellion against God led to grief, pain, and death. We also learn of the emergence of deep fractures in human relationships. For example, how differences between the two brothers, Cain and Abel, resulted in Cain murdering Abel. We learn that Cain subsequently built a city where violence and oppression were the order of the day.

We then encounter King Lamech, the first man in the Bible to marry more than one wife and who boasted that his cruelty made that of Cain pale into insignificance. We also see the emergence of various other Kings who married many wives and whose reigns were characterized by evil and corruption.

During that time, people ignored God. We are told that humanity's wickedness caused God a lot of grief. Because of that, God decided to unleash a great flood to wash the world of sin. Noah and his family were spared from this punishment because of Noah's obedience and faithfulness to God.

We learn that after the flood, Noah was commissioned to go into the world. His sons Shem, Ham, and Japheth gave birth to many children scattered across many parts of the world.

A key theme of the stories thus far is that God kept giving humanity a chance. However, humanity's wickedness and sinfulness did not cease, except for a handful of people, one of whom was Abraham. God promised Abraham that he would give him a great nation as part of God's plan to rescue a rebellious world.

Unfortunately, Abraham was advancing in age and did not have any children. His wife, Sarah, was also getting old and barren. Abraham pleaded with God to give him a child—a child who would inherit his estate. God responded and promised Abraham to expect to beget a son. Further, God promised Abraham that his offspring would be in large numbers, as the stars in the heavens (Genesis 15:2- 5).

Meanwhile, out of apparent despair and desperation, Sarah suggested to Abraham that he should sleep with their Egyptian maidservant Hagar so he could at least have a child to whom he could bequeath an inheritance. Hagar conceived a boy child, Ishmael (Genesis 16:1-4).

Later, God fulfilled his promise to Abraham. Sarah, who was 90 years old, conceived a boy, Isaac. However, a few years later, in an unexpected turn of events, God asked Abraham to sacrifice Isaac as a burnt offering (Genesis 22: 1–19).

The Ultimate Test of Faith

For a reasonable human being whose life is guided by human logic, it would have been difficult to obey these instructions from God. The thought process would probably have gone like this:

First, by asking me to kill my only son and offer him as a sacrifice, God would contradict his promise that I would beget many children and become the father of many nations. Secondly, by asking me to kill my innocent son, God would be asking me to do an exceptionally unjust act. Thirdly, killing my only son would be a heartless act that would cause me and Sarah endless torment and anguish (Hicks, 2019).

However, Abraham did not falter in his obedience and faith in God despite the apparent agony. And just as he was about to kill his son, an angel of God called him from heaven and asked him not to do anything to his son (Genesis 22: 1–19).

Abraham passed the test of faith in God through his unquestioning obedience that defied reason.[215] God, in turn, fulfilled his covenant with Abraham. Abraham's actions in these circumstances demonstrate to us an immensely courageous and bold act of faith.

Chapter 11

Example of Faith in Action

*"None of us knows what might happen
even the next minute, yet still we go
forward. Because we trust. Because we
have Faith."*
—Paul Coelho

IT IS EASY TO TALK and hypothesize about different aspects of faith. However, the real test of faith occurs in our daily lives. In this chapter, I have given an example from my experience that hopefully should shed light on how God can intervene or manifest Himself in our lives if we have faith - a case for enhancing our faith in Him.

◆◆◆

A Challenging Encounter in Dar-es-Salaam

As a young man, my biggest hope was to pursue a career in accountancy and set up an accountancy firm to become my "own" boss. However, I joined a major international company that offered me much more fulfillment than I expected. The thoughts of private practice vanished.

In 1983, shortly after joining the multinational company, my employer asked me to travel to Dar-es-Salaam, Tanzania, on a business assignment. This trip was to be my first time out of the country and my first time flying in an aircraft. It was a truly memorable trip but for the wrong reasons.

I went to Dar-es-Salaam on a Wednesday and planned to return to Nairobi the following Sunday. My assignment was quite simple. I finished it in a day and had much spare time before returning to Nairobi.

Full of excitement, I set out on a tour of Dar-es-Salaam at around 9:00 a.m. on Friday, armed with my camera. After walking around for about an hour, I saw a very nice-looking building, *Nyumba ya Sanaa*. I decided to take some photos of it.

However, no sooner had I started taking the pictures than a Land Rover passing by carrying some soldiers screeched to a halt. Two soldiers immediately jumped out of the back of the vehicle and headed toward me. They accused me of taking photos in a prohibited area.

They roughed me up and confiscated my camera. They forced me onto the back of the vehicle and sped off. I had no idea where they were taking me.

After about 20 minutes, we arrived at a military barracks. The place was full of mean-looking soldiers. My arrival there was a bit of a spectacle. I recall some soldiers uttering unpleasant words as I alighted from the Land Rover. I was the center of attraction.

It is worth mentioning that this event happened when the relationship between Tanzania and Kenya was at a low ebb, a factor that did not augur well for me at the hands of the soldiers.

I was frog-marched into a small room within the military barracks, where I was locked up. The situation seemed quite ominous, but I believed God would ultimately come to my rescue.

After about four hours, which seemed like a lifetime, a soldier who appeared to be a senior of the ones I had interacted with earlier came into the room. He told me they wanted to view all the photographs I had taken with my camera. However, because the technicians within the barracks did not have the equipment to process color film, they would have to hand me over to the police at the Central Police Station in Dar-es-Salaam, where I would stay in custody until they found somebody who could process the film.

A short while later, I was huddled into another Land Rover and taken to the Central Police Station, guarded by two soldiers. When we arrived, the police officer in charge of the station was not there. It seemed that the police had to follow a particular protocol when the military handed over somebody for detention.

After waiting for some time, the soldiers became jittery. They spoke with one of the police officers and agreed that the soldiers would depart and contact the police officers later. Meanwhile, I was to be locked up in the cells until the police officer in charge of the station showed up.

Shortly after that, the police officer in charge of the station walked in. I knew my fate was sealed at that point, and only divine intervention could save me.

To my amazement, when the matter was explained to the police officer in charge of the station, and I finished telling him my side of the story, he said that I had not committed any crime. He added that photographing *Nyumba ya Sanaa* was not prohibited because it was not a military facility. He asked the police officers there to release me immediately. He requested that I leave my passport at the police station for retrieval the following day when the soldiers were expected to have finished processing the film.

I will never forget the intense feeling of freedom I felt as I left the police station. That day, I realized the real value of freedom. As the adage goes, sometimes you do not appreciate what you have until you lose it.

As I left the police station, I did not even want to look back in case someone asked me to go back for additional interrogation. It took me about fifteen minutes to walk from the police station to the hotel, but it felt like two endless hours.

I spent the rest of the day in my hotel room, relaxing from my bizarre ordeal. I hoped the military would not come up with something else that would create further complications. I could hardly sleep that night.

The following morning, at around 9:00 am, I went to the police station to collect my passport and camera. It was an awkward moment. I did not know how things would unfold and hoped for the best.

The policeman on duty was very pleasant and professional. He handed me my passport. The military had still not found someone to process the film, so he asked me to return to the police station later to check for my camera.

I did not bother to go back to retrieve the camera. At that point, it did not have any meaningful value to me. I flew back to Nairobi the following day.

Whenever I reflect on this incident, which in hindsight may seem trivial, I see the hand of God working in a big way. In my eyes, the senior police officer at the Central Police Station in Dar-es-Salaam was a vessel of God. I needed not to beget a child as the Biblical Abraham desired but to be free, and God answered my prayers.

Chapter 12

Enhancing our Faith in God

*"Be on guard. Stand firm in the faith. Be
courageous. Be strong."*
— 1 Corinthians 16:13

LIVING IN FAITH MEANS DEMONSTRATING our obedience to God with actions. To this end, we need to show our contentment with the blessings that God has given us. Many disputes arise between us and others because of our constant quest to accumulate material possessions and a perpetual desire for pleasure. We should avoid being too attached to the material things of the world lest the emptiness of it all befall us, as vividly described by the teacher in the book of Ecclesiastes in the Old Testament of the Bible.[216]

> *⁷ I acquired male and female servants, and had servants born in my house. Yes, I had greater possessions of herds and flocks than all who were in Jerusalem before me. ⁸ I also gathered for myself silver and gold and the special treasures of kings and of the provinces. I acquired male and female singers, the delights of the sons of men, and musical instruments of all kinds.*
> *⁹ So I became great and excelled more than all who were before me in Jerusalem. Also my wisdom remained with me.*
> *¹⁰ Whatever my eyes desired I did not keep from them.*
> *I did not withhold my heart from any pleasure,*
> *For my heart rejoiced in all my labor;*
> *And this was my reward from all my labor.*
> *¹¹ Then I looked on all the works that my hands had done*
> *And on the labor in which I had toiled;*
> *And indeed all was vanity and grasping for the wind.*
> *There was no profit under the sun. (Ecclesiastes 2:7-11)*

We must love the Lord our God and others as we love ourselves (Mark 12: 30-31). Demonstrating our love means investing quality time to build our relationship with God through prayer, reading scripture, and worshiping God with others. Loving our neighbors means extending our hand of friendship to them and using our resources to serve them to the best of our ability.

We should also show joy in God. This requires maintaining a positive attitude to promote a positive image of our Lord God and his followers (Philippians 4:4).

We should strive for peace despite the many trials and tribulations we will encounter (Mathew 5:9).

Living in faith also means showing kindness to others. It means demonstrating, with actions, our obedience to God. To this end, we need to demonstrate our contentment with the blessings God has bestowed upon us.

Steps in Enhancing our Faith in God

The first step in enhancing our faith in God is to begin our journey in faith from our current position. Others may have nurtured their faith for a long time and are significantly ahead of us. This should not discourage us. Faith in God is personal. We should start from wherever we are, consistently maintaining a positive attitude about our faith and relentlessly seeking God's guidance to grow our faith in Him.

The second step is to read the word of God regularly. "Faith comes by hearing, and hearing by the word of God" (Romans 10:17). Regularly reading the word of God will help us grow in faith.[217]

A Golfing Adventure

In April 2023, my close friend and former schoolmate, Charles Ngarama Kamau, invited me for tea at the VetLab Sports Club, which is nestled within the University of Nairobi Veterinary Medicine Campus at Kabete. We hadn't caught up in ages, and I was eager to meet him to discuss our experiences in semi-retirement.

Upon arriving at the club, I was struck by its popularity. People flocked there for various reasons—some hit the gym, others hit golf balls, and many, like Charles, enjoyed relaxing and socializing. Charles was with his brother Mbugua Kamau, a man with an exceptional gift of the gab and one of the most humorous people I've ever met.

We spent about four hours reminiscing about our high school days and laughing about our youthful escapades. It's true what they say—laughter is the best medicine. That short social interaction felt like a tonic, rejuvenating us all.

During that memorable evening, Charles and Mbugua, with their characteristic enthusiasm, offered to sponsor me to join the club. They asked a club employee to explain the joining procedures and hand me an application form. I completed the initial formalities that evening thanks to their dynamism and support.

The next day, I returned to the club to deliver the documents it needed to support my application. A few days later, the club's administrator invited me to interview with the Club's Board of Directors.

Charles and Mbugua introduced me to the Club's Board of Directors in the most robust way imaginable, and soon after, the Board accepted me as a club member. And thus began my fascinating journey into the world of golf—a sport unlike any other.

Initially, I naively thought golf was just about getting clubs and balls and striking the ball from one point of the golf course to another. Of course, that is the essence of the game, but I quickly realized there was much more to it than I had ever imagined.

My first step was to procure golf equipment. Simple enough, right? Wrong.

The list of standard golf paraphernalia can be pretty intimidating. You need golf clubs, golf balls, a special glove to prevent blisters, tees to elevate the ball, special shoes with spikes for stability, a golf cap, a collared shirt, ball markers, a towel—the list goes on. And that's just the essentials!

A standard golf bag contains 14 clubs, each with a different length and head shape, each serving a unique purpose. Learning the "true" purpose of each club was humbling. For example, I learned that variables such as distance and the nature of the ground (the "lie") affect the efficiency of making a golf ball move from point A to point B. Hence, different clubs are needed, each designed to handle specific scenarios on the golf course.

But owning a nice set of clubs doesn't guarantee you'll be a good player. You need to practice, practice, and practice—preferably under the guidance of an experienced golfer or coach.

Even here, potential hurdles abound. For example, during my continuing golfing journey, an experienced golfer told me my game suffered because my clubs were too long for my body size. Imagine my shock, considering that just four months earlier, another professional had convinced me to have all my clubs elongated to improve my swing! Welcome to the endless learning curve of golf.

Those who have never played golf might wonder how golfers handle all that equipment. While carrying a golf bag or pulling it on a cart is possible, most prefer to use a caddy.

A caddy does more than carry the bag; they provide feedback on your performance, advise on your next move, and sometimes even become a friend and mentor. Plus, they'll gladly remind you to keep your shirt tucked in and your cell phone off—a golfer's version of sacred commandments!

When I started learning the game's vocabulary, it sounded like the language of bird-watching enthusiasts. I heard words like birdie, eagle, double-eagle, albatross, turkey, dogleg, and chicken wing.

Who, other than a golfer, can claim to have ever seen a birdie (not bird), a double-eagle, or a dogleg?

Other intriguing terms included bunker, hook, slice, stinger, bogey, double-bogey, fairway, rough, tee box, and handicap. Handicap? Yes, handicap! These words were mystifying at first, but I soon learned they were part of the essential language spoken by those in the golfing community.

In soccer, the more goals you score, the better you perform. The same applies to many sports. But in golf, things are delightfully upside down. The more points you score, the worse your performance! In other words, the fewer strokes you take to get the ball from start to finish, the better.

But there is a nice twist to the golf's scoring system: it works in such a way that it levels the playing field. It undoubtedly makes golf the most equitable sport on earth. Strangely, it's a sport beloved in capitalist countries, yet it has all the markings of socialism.

This is how the scoring system works: Newcomers and those with less experience get credit (a handicap) to recognize their "inexperience." This handicap is factored into the net score, meaning even a relatively inexperienced player can win a game. I managed it once, and the feeling was nothing short of euphoric!

Every sport has rules, and golf is no exception. However, unlike soccer, where you can play with just a few basic rules, golf requires you to learn a gazillion rules (the Official Rules), which fall under 25 categories.[218] You even have to pass a test before being allowed to play in an official competition.

And when you start playing, the game can be pretty exciting. But "golf" and "excitement" might seem contradictory to the uninitiated. After all, when you visit a golf course, you'll see small groups of people hitting golf balls, then walking toward the balls and hitting them again until they reach a hole. And they repeat this routine multiple times. Boring, right? No.

Believe it or not, the game can be pretty nerve-wracking and exciting. If you need proof, watch one of the international tournaments on YouTube, especially the action at the final hole. You might be surprised by the frenzy that erupts when a player sinks the ball.

Once you understand the game, its appeal and excitement become almost irresistible. It can even become addictive—but in a positive way!

There's something about the "whish" of a well-hit ball soaring through the air toward the green that's almost indescribable - every golfer dreams of consistently achieving the perfect golf swing. After my short stint as a player, I've concluded that the quest for this consistency is one of the reasons golf is so addictive.

The internet contains videos from golf experts offering tips on achieving the perfect swing. But no matter how hard I try to apply some of these ideas, I've never mastered them. When I think I've cracked the secret, I find another video with more tips and tricks.

On the surface, one might wonder why achieving the perfect swing is so hard. But in reality, it's both an art and a science, dependent on variables like stance, lie, wind direction, club choice, body flexibility, and distance to the target. The endless pursuit of the perfect swing is part of what gives golf its unique flavor.

But there is another serious and important side to golf: its benefits. The most significant benefit I've found in golf is its positive impact on health. By the time you finish playing a round of golf, covering all 18 holes, you'll have walked anywhere between six and twelve kilometers, depending on the course. The walk is in open spaces, on manicured lawns, surrounded by trees. It's refreshing, good for the heart, and helps improve fitness, weight loss, muscle tone, and endurance.

Golf can also help reduce stress and enhance connections with friends and community.

Golf is unique because it can be played individually or with others. It is also a game for everyone, regardless of age or gender – an inclusive sport that individuals of all abilities can enjoy.

Drawing Parallels with the Christian Faith

What does it take to become a golfer, enjoy the game, and eventually become good at it? The answers might seem obvious: You need to join a golf club, get the right equipment, learn how to play, understand the rules, learn the terminology, grasp the scoring system, and play regularly. It would help if you also played with others, regardless of their age, gender, or station in life. And, of course, a good caddy can make all the difference.

Now, what does it take to become a Christian, to enjoy your faith, and to grow spiritually? The answer is surprisingly similar.

To start, you only need one essential piece of equipment—the Bible. Other supplementary tools, like hymn books, can be helpful, but you don't need special attire, spiked shoes, or a bag of paraphernalia. You don't need a handicap, either. You become a Christian just as you are. And like golf, Christianity is for everyone—children, adults, boys, girls, and seniors alike. Everyone is welcome to join.

Perfection is elusive in both golf and faith. As Christians, we must always pray before God, seeking forgiveness for our deficiencies and blessings to become better believers.

As golf requires dedication, practice, and the proper guidance to improve, so does our Christian journey. We are called to "press on toward the goal to win the prize for which God has called [us] heavenward in Christ Jesus" **(Philippians 3:14, NIV)**.

Like golfers pursuing the perfect swing, our spiritual walk is a continuous process of growth and learning. Just as golfers need a caddy for support and guidance, we also have a constant guide in our faith journey—God's Word.

Proverbs 3:5-6 (NIV) reminds us, "Trust in the Lord with all your heart and lean not on your own understanding; in all your ways submit to him, and he will make your paths straight." By relying on God, embracing fellowship with others, and persevering through challenges, we can grow as golfers and as Christians, ever striving toward the ultimate prize of eternal life with Christ.

"A History of the Bible: Who Wrote It and When?"
HistoryExtra, September 10, 2019.
https://www.historyextra.com/period/ancient-
history/history-bible-origins-who-wrote-when-how-
reliable-historical-record/.

"Afghan Conflict: US and Taliban Sign Deal to End 18-Year
War." BBC News. BBC, February 29, 2020.
https://www.bbc.com/news/world-asia-51689443.

"Al-Qur'an Al-Kareem - القرآن الكريم." Surah Al-Kafirun [109:6].
Accessed April 2, 2020. https://Quran.com/109/6.

Better Health Channel. "Golf - health benefits," n.d.
https://www.betterhealth.vic.gov.au/health/healthylivi
ng/golf-health-benefits#health-benefits-of-golf.

"COFFEE DEVELOPMENT AND MARKETING STRATEGY 2024-
2029," 2024. https://kilimo.go.ke/wp-
content/uploads/2024/03/Final-Draft-Coffee-
Developemnt-and-Marketing-Strategy-27-Jan-2024-
1.pdf.

"Early Buddhism: Three Baskets of Dharma." *Dharma*, 2017,
34–59. https://doi.org/10.1515/9780824860639-006.

"Funny Philosophers Jokes." WorkJoke Profession Jokes.
Accessed April 7, 2020.

"Hadith and the Corruption of the Great Religion of Islam:
Submission.org - Your Best Source for Submission
(Islam)." Hadith and the Corruption of the great
religion of Islam | Submission.org - Your best source
for Submission (Islam). Accessed April 2, 2020.
https://submission.org/Corruption_of_Religion.html.

"Introduction to the Bible and Biblical Problems." The Secular
        Web. Accessed March 31, 2020.
        https://infidels.org/library/modern/donald_morgan/in
        tro.html

"Nigeria People 2020." Nigeria People 2020, CIA World
        Factbook. Accessed April 26, 2020.
        https://theodora.com/wfbcurrent/nigeria/nigeria_peop
        le.html.

"PCEA Church's Attack on Gikuyu Culture Is Wrong."
        kenya2uhub, May 29, 2018.
        https://www.kenya2uhub.com/plots-houses-property-
        apartments/pcea-churchs-attack-on-gikuyu-culture-
        is-wrong/.

"QuranX.com The Most Complete Quran / Hadith / Tafsir
        Collection Available!" Sahih Bukhari Hadiths. Accessed
        April 10, 2020. https://quranx.com/hadith/Bukhari/In-
        Book/Book-5/Hadith-21/.

"QuranX.com The Most Complete Quran / Hadith / Tafsir
        Collection Available!" Sahih Bukhari Hadiths. Accessed
        April 10, 2020. https://quranx.com/hadith/Bukhari/In-
        Book/Book-59/Hadith-83/.

"QuranX.com The Most Complete Quran / Hadith / Tafsir
        Collection Available!" Sahih Bukhari Hadiths. Accessed
        April 10, 2020. https://quranx.com/hadith/Bukhari/In-
        Book/Book-59/Hadith-74/.

"QuranX.com The Most Complete Quran / Hadith / Tafsir
        Collection Available!" Sahih Bukhari Hadiths. Accessed
        April 10, 2020. https://quranx.com/hadith/Bukhari/In-
        Book/Book-67/Hadith-6/.

"QuranX.com The Most Complete Quran / Hadith / Tafsir
        Collection Available!" Sahih Bukhari Hadiths. Accessed
        April 10, 2020. https://quranx.com/hadith/Bukhari/In-
        Book/Book-67/Hadith-31/.

"QuranX.com The Most Complete Quran / Hadith / Tafsir
        Collection Available!" Sahih Bukhari Hadiths. Accessed
        April 10, 2020. https://quranx.com/hadith/Bukhari/In-
        Book/Book-67/Hadith-127/.

"QuranX.com The Most Complete Quran / Hadith / Tafsir
    Collection Available!" Sahih Bukhari Hadiths. Accessed
    April 10, 2020. https://quranx.com/hadith/Bukhari/In-
    Book/Book-77/Hadith-165/.
"Religions - Christianity: The Basics of Christian Beliefs." BBC.
    BBC, August 14, 2009.
    https://www.bbc.co.uk/religion/religions/christianity/b
    eliefs/basics_1.shtml.
"Religious Composition by Country, 2010-2050." Pew Research
    Center's Religion & Public Life Project, December 31,
    2019.
    https://www.pewforum.org/2015/04/02/religious-
    projection-table/2020/number/all/.
"The Gita's Setting Reflects Not Logical Absurdity but
    Metaphysical Urgency." Begin each day enriched with
    nuggets of timeless wisdom. Article By Chaitanya
    Charan Das. Accessed April 11, 2020.
    https://www.gitadaily.com/the-gitas-setting-reflects-
    not-logical-absurdity-but-metaphysical-urgency/.
"The Teaching of the Bhagavad Gita." Comparative Religion -
    Possible difficulties in the philosophy of the Bhagavad
    Gita. Accessed April 10, 2020.
"Why Don't We Possess Any of the Original Manuscripts of the
    Books of the Bible? by Don Stewart." Blue Letter Bible.
    Accessed April 22, 2020.
    https://www.blueletterbible.org/Comm/stewart_don/fa
    q/words-bible/question4-original-manuscripts-of-
    the-bible.cfm.
Abeysekara, Ananda. "The Saffron Army, Violence, Terror(ism):
    Buddhism, Identity, and Difference in Sri
    Lanka." *Numen* 48, no. 1 (2001): 1-46. Accessed April 11,
    2020. www.jstor.org/stable/3270564.
Basu, Anindita. "Mahabharata." Ancient History Encyclopedia.
    Ancient History Encyclopedia, April 20, 2020.
    https://www.ancient.eu/Mahabharata/.
Beyers, Jaco. "Religion and Culture: Revisiting a Close
    Relative." *HTS Teologiese Studies / Theological Studies* 73,
    no. 1 (2017). https://doi.org/10.4102/hts.v73i1.3864.

Bezhan, Frud. "Afghans Lift Lid On Sports Under The Taliban." RadioFreeEurope/RadioLiberty. Radio Free Europe / Radio Liberty, July 11, 2012. https://www.rferl.org/a/afghans-recall-sports-under-the-taliban/24642278.html.

Billy Graham Evangelic Association (2015). 9 Ways to Grow in Your Faith. *Retrieved on 28 June 2019 from https://billygraham.org/story/9-ways-to-grow-in-your-faith/*

Brooks, Alison Wood, and Leslie K. John. "How to Ask Great Questions." Harvard Business Review, November 19, 2019. https://hbr.org/2018/05/the-surprising-power-of-questions.

Brown, Daniel. *Rethinking Tradition in Modern Islamic Thought.* New York: Cambridge, 1998.

Craig, William Lane., and Quentin Smith. *Theism, Atheism, and Big Bang Cosmology.* Oxford: Clarendon Press, 1993.

Dashti, Ali. *Twenty Three Years: a Study of the Prophetic Career of Mohammed.* People International, 1990.

Del Soldato, Eva. "Natural Philosophy in the Renaissance." Stanford Encyclopedia of Philosophy. Stanford University, April 8, 2019. https://plato.stanford.edu/entries/natphil-ren/.

El-Neil, Ibn. *The Truth About Islam.* New York, NY: Eloquent Books, 2008.

Ferr, Frederick. *Basic Modern Philosophy of Religion.* Place of publication not identified: Routledge, 2016.

Fitzgerald, Timothy. *Discourse on Civility and Barbarity.* New York: Oxford University Press, 2012.

Gathogo, Julius. "The Continuity of Indigenous Rituals in African Ecclesiology: A Kenyan Experience from a Historical Perspective." *STJ | Stellenbosch Theological Journal* 3, no. 1 (2017). https://doi.org/10.17570/stj.2017.v3n1.a06.

George, Alison. "Kopimism: The World's Newest Religion Explained." New Scientist, January 6, 2012. https://www.newscientist.com/article/dn21334-kopimism-the-worlds-newest-religion-explained/.

Hagin, K.E. (2019). How to Increase Your Faith. *Retrieved on 28 June 2019 from https://www.rhema.org/index.php?option=com_content&vie w=article&id=1030:how-to-increase-your-faith&catid=46&Itemid=141*

Hick, John. *Philosophy of Religion*. Englewood Cliffs, NJ: Prentice-Hall, 1990.

Hicks, S. (2019). Faith: The Story of Abraham. *Retrieved on 28 June 2019 from https://www.youtube.com/watch?v=4iEAOtZMS3Q&list=PL5 CB5A1E2D9F4E6A2&index=24*

Islam, J.A. (2020). The Difference Between Hadith and Sunna. Retrieved on 2 April 2020 from http://quransmessage.com/articles/hadith%20and%20 sunna%20FM3.htm.

Jerryson, Michael K., and Mark Juergensmeyer. *Buddhist Warfare*. Oxford: Oxford University Press, 2010.

Jordan, R.B. (2012). Three Ways to Increase Your Faith. Retrieved *on 28 June 2019* from https://www.crosswalk.com/faith/spiritual-life/three-ways-to-increase-your-faith.html

Kenyatta, Jomo, and B. Malinowski. *Facing Mount Kenya*. New York: AMS Press, 1978

Kiongo, C, and I C Dougall. "14/The Bible-1." Essay. In *What I Believe*, edited by J O Welsh, 36–37. Nairobi, Kenya: PCEA Jitegemea Publishers, 2009.

Komu, Nicholas. "PCEA Ban on Kikuyu Rite Sparks Storm." PCEA ban on Kikuyu rite sparks big storm. Daily Nation, May 24, 2018. https://mobile.nation.co.ke/news/PCEA-ban-on-Kikuyu-rite-sparks-big-storm/1950946-4577196-3rttsfz/index.html.

Lexico Dictionary. Retrieved from https://www.lexico.com/en/definition/faith

Mbiti, John S. *African Religions & Philosophy*. Oxford: Heinemann, 2006.

Meister, Chad. "Philosophy of Religion." Internet Encyclopedia
        of Philosophy. Accessed April 5, 2020.
        https://www.iep.utm.edu/religion/.
Mill, John Stuart. *Utilitarianism ; Liberty*. London: Dent, 1972.
Ngugi, Muiru. "Modern Christian Life and Kikuyu Rituals."
        Medium. Medium, December 22, 2019.
        https://medium.com/@muirucngugi/modern-
        christian-life-and-kikuyu-rituals-433656d95f5d.
Ngwiri, Magesha. "NGWIRI: Church Should Clean House First
        before Chasing Harmless." Daily Nation. Daily Nation,
        June 1, 2018.
        https://www.nation.co.ke/oped/opinion/Church-
        should-clean-house-first/440808-4590866-
        hm2ghwz/index.html.
Okeke, Chukwuma O., Christopher N. Ibenwa, and Gloria
        Tochukwu Okeke. "Conflicts Between African
        Traditional Religion and Christianity in Eastern
        Nigeria: The Igbo Example." *SAGE Open* 7, no. 2 (2017):
        215824401770932.
        https://doi.org/10.1177/21582440017709322.
Okeke, Henry Chukwudi. The *Spirituality of the Igbo People of
        Nigeria an Example of Religious Modernization in a Global
        World*. S.l.: LIT VERLAG, 2020.
Presbyterian Church of East Africa - World Council of
        Churches, September 25, 2013.
        https://www.oikoumene.org/en/member-
        churches/presbyterian-church-of-east-africa.
Rathje, W. "Why the Taliban Are Destroying Buddhas." USA
        Today. Gannett Satellite Information Network.
        Accessed April 26, 2020.
        https://usatoday30.usatoday.com/news/science/archae
        ology/2001-03-22-afghan-buddhas.htm.
Reichenbach, Bruce. "Cosmological Argument." Stanford
        Encyclopedia of Philosophy. Stanford University,
        October 11, 2017.
        https://plato.stanford.edu/entries/cosmological-
        argument/.

Romig, Rollo. "The First Church of Pirate Bay." The New
    Yorker. The New Yorker, June 18, 2017.
    https://www.newyorker.com/culture/culture-desk/the-
    first-church-of-pirate-bay.

Roy, Arundhati. "The Disconnect between Religion and
    Culture." Eurozine, August 20, 2015.
    https://www.eurozine.com/the-disconnect-between-
    religion-and-culture/.

Runzo, Joseph. "God, Commitment, and Other Faiths:
    Pluralism vs Relativism." *World Views and Perceiving
    God*, 1993, 193–218. https://doi.org/10.1007/978-1-349-
    23106-5_9.

Sasaki, Joni Y., and Heejung S. Kim. "At the Intersection of
    Culture and Religion: A Cultural Analysis of Religion's
    Implications for Secondary Control and Social
    Affiliation." *Journal of Personality and Social Psychology*
    101, no. 2 (2011): 401–14.
    https://doi.org/10.1037/a0021849.

Seife, C. (2000). The Vatican regrets burning cosmologist.
    *Science Now. Archived from the original on 8 June 2013.
    Retrieved 28 June 2019.*

Shankar, Ravi. "Contradictions in the Gita Helps One to Think -
    Times of India." The Times of India. The Times of
    India, December 23, 2009.
    https://timesofindia.indiatimes.com/Contradictions-
    in-the-Gita-helps-one-to-
    think/articleshow/4910701.cms.

Shell-Duncan, Bettina, David Gathara, and Zhuzhi Moore.
    "Female Genital Mutilation/Cutting in Kenya: Is Change
    Taking Place? Descriptive Statistics from Four Waves of
    Demographic and Health Surveys," 2017.
    https://doi.org/10.31899/rh7.1022.

Sherwood, Harriet. "Religion: Why Faith Is Becoming More and
    More Popular." The Guardian. Guardian News and
    Media, August 27, 2018.
    https://www.theguardian.com/news/2018/aug/27/religi
    on-why-is-faith-growing-and-what-happens-next

Soka Gakkai International. "The Enlightenment of Women."
    Soka Gakkai International (SGI), July 17, 2008.
    https://www.sgi.org/about-us/buddhist-concepts/the-
    enlightenment-of-women.html.
The Cambridge History of Islam. Cambridge: Cambridge Univ.
    Press, 1980.
The Editors of Encyclopaedia Britannica. "Pali Canon."
    Encyclopædia Britannica. Encyclopædia Britannica,
    inc., March 22, 2019.
    https://www.britannica.com/topic/Tipitaka.
"The Official Rules of Golf," R&A, n.d.,
    https://www.randa.org/rog/the-rules-of-golf.
Tierney, James. "The Apostles' Creed." Cardinal Newman Faith
    Resources Inc, October 7, 2008.
    https://www.cardinalnewman.com.au/downloads.
Timmons, Greg. "Muhammad." Biography.com. A&E Networks
    Television, November 5, 2019.
    https://www.biography.com/religious-
    figure/muhammad.
Urdang, Laurence. *The Oxford Desk Dictionary.* New York: Oxford
    University Press, 1995.
User, Super. "Chronology History." www.pcea.or.ke. Accessed
    April 14, 2020. http://www.pcea.or.ke/index.php/helix-
    framework-6.
Violatti, Cristian. "The Vedas." Ancient History Encyclopedia.
    Ancient History Encyclopedia, April 8, 2020.
    https://www.ancient.eu/The_Vedas/.
Warraq, Ibn. *Why I Am Not a Muslim.* Amherst, NY: Prometheus
    Books, 2003.
What Is Hinduism? Cogito, 2019.
    https://www.youtube.com/watch?v=xlBEEuYIWwY.
"Who Are the Taliban?" BBC News. BBC, February 27, 2020.
    https://www.bbc.com/news/world-south-asia-
    11451718.
"English." Kopimistsamfundet. Accessed March 30, 2020.
    http://kopimistsamfundet.se/english/.
Church of the Flying Spaghetti Monster. Accessed March 30,
    2020. https://www.spaghettimonster.org/.

Pecorino, Philip A. *Online Textbook*. Accessed March 30, 2020.
	https://www.qcc.cuny.edu/SocialSciences/ppecorino/PHIL_of_RELIGION_TEXT/default.htm

"Hinduism." Sacred. Accessed April 3, 2020.
	https://www.sacred-texts.com/hin/index.htm.

"Donald Morgan." The Secular Web. Accessed April 7, 2020.
	https://infidels.org/library/modern/donald_morgan/.

"Abrogation In The Koran - Muhammadanism." Accessed April 9, 2020.
	http://www.muhammadanism.org/Quran/abrogation_koran.pdf.Admin. "Philosophy Jokes." Puns And One Liners, November 20, 2015.
	https://punsandoneliners.com/randomness/philosophy-jokes/.

"Why I Am Not a Hindu." The Secular Web. Accessed April 10, 2020.
	https://infidels.org/library/modern/ramendra_nath/hindu.html.

"Pāli Canon." Wikiwand. Accessed April 11, 2020.
	https://www.wikiwand.com/en/P%C4%81li_Canon.

"Chronology History." www.pcea.or.ke. Accessed April 15, 2020. http://www.pcea.or.ke/index.php/helix-framework-6.

Faith: The Story of Abraham". YouTube video. 8.51. "Stephen Hicks." February 8, 2010.
	https://www.youtube.com/watch?v=4iEAOtZMS3Q&list=PL5CB5A1E2D9F4E6A2&index=24.

Holy Books: The Qur'an. YouTube video. 10.04. A film by Kim Roden. April 20, 2018.
	https://www.youtube.com/watch?v=ABkhC-QHG34&t=327s.

Bosworth, F.F. (2019). F. F. Bosworth Quotes. *Retrieved on 28 June 2019 from https://www.azquotes.com/author/23237-F_F_Bosworth*

"Religions - Islam: Basic Articles of Faith." BBC. BBC, July 19, 2011.
	https://www.bbc.co.uk/religion/religions/islam/beliefs/beliefs.shtml.

Notes

1 "Religious Composition by Country, 2010-2050." Pew Research Center's Religion & Public Life Project, December 31, 2019. https://www.pewforum.org/2015/04/02/religious-projection-table/2020/number/all/.

2 Mbiti, John S. *African Religions & Philosophy*. Oxford: Heinemann, 2006.

3 Gathogo, Julius. "The Continuity of Indigenous Rituals in African Ecclesiology: A Kenyan Experience from a Historical Perspective." *STJ | Stellenbosch Theological Journal* 3, no. 1 (2017). https://doi.org/10.17570/stj.2017.v3n1.a06.

4 Mbiti, John S. *African Religions & Philosophy*. Oxford: Heinemann, 2006.

5 Ferr, Frederick. *Basic Modern Philosophy of Religion*. Place of publication not identified: Routledge, 2016.

6 Urdang, Laurence. *The Oxford Desk Dictionary*. New York: Oxford University Press, 1995.

7 "Religious Composition by Country, 2010-2050." Pew Research Center's Religion & Public Life Project, December 31, 2019. https://www.pewforum.org/2015/04/02/religious-projection-table/2020/number/all/.

8 Sherwood, Harriet. "Religion: Why Faith Is Becoming More and More Popular." The Guardian. Guardian News and Media, August 27, 2018. https://www.theguardian.com/news/2018/aug/27/religion-why-is-faith-growing-and-what-happens-next

---

9 "Religious Composition by Country, 2010-2050." Pew
     Research Center's Religion & Public Life Project,
     December 31, 2019.
     https://www.pewforum.org/2015/04/02/religious-
     projection-table/2020/number/all/.

10 Ibid
11 Ibid
12 Ibid
13 Pecorino, Philip A. *Online Textbook*. Accessed March 30, 2020.
     https://www.qcc.cuny.edu/SocialSciences/ppecorino/PHIL
     _of_RELIGION_TEXT/TABLE_of_CONTENTS.htm.
14 Sherwood, Harriet. "Religion: Why Faith Is Becoming More
     and More Popular." The Guardian. Guardian News and
     Media, August 27, 2018.
     https://www.theguardian.com/news/2018/aug/27/religion
     -why-is-faith-growing-and-what-happens-next
15 Ibid
16 Ibid
17 Ibid
18 Ibid
19 George, Alison. "Kopimism: The World's Newest Religion
     Explained." New Scientist, January 6, 2012.
     https://www.newscientist.com/article/dn21334-
     kopimism-the-worlds-newest-religion-explained/.
20 "English." Kopimistsamfundet. Accessed March 30, 2020.
     http://kopimistsamfundet.se/english/.
21 Romig, Rollo. "The First Church of Pirate Bay." The New
     Yorker. The New Yorker, June 18, 2017.
     https://www.newyorker.com/culture/culture-desk/the-
     first-church-of-pirate-bay.
22 Church of the Flying Spaghetti Monster. Accessed March 30,
     2020. https://www.spaghettimonster.org/.
23 "A History of the Bible: Who Wrote It and When?"
     HistoryExtra, September 10, 2019.
     https://www.historyextra.com/period/ancient-
     history/history-bible-origins-who-wrote-when-how-
     reliable-historical-record/.

---

24 "Introduction to the Bible and Biblical Problems." The
     Secular Web. Accessed March 31, 2020.
     https://infidels.org/library/modern/donald_morgan/intr
     o.html

25 Kiongo, C, and I C Dougall. "14/The Bible-1." Essay. In *What I
     Believe*, edited by J O Welsh, 36–37. Nairobi, Kenya: PCEA
     Jitegemea Publishers, 2009.

26 "Why Don't We Possess Any of the Original Manuscripts of
     the Books of the Bible? by Don Stewart." Blue Letter
     Bible. Accessed April 22, 2020.
     https://www.blueletterbible.org/Comm/stewart_don/faq
     /words-bible/question4-original-manuscripts-of-the-
     bible.cfm.

27 "A History of the Bible: Who Wrote It and When?"
     HistoryExtra, September 10, 2019.
     https://www.historyextra.com/period/ancient-
     history/history-bible-origins-who-wrote-when-how-
     reliable-historical-record/.

28 Ibid

29 Ibid

30 Ibid

31 Ibid

32 Ibid

33 Ibid

34 "Religions - Christianity: The Basics of Christian Beliefs."
     BBC. BBC, August 14, 2009.
     https://www.bbc.co.uk/religion/religions/christianity/beli
     efs/basics_1.shtml.

35 Ibid.

36 Ibid.

37 Kiongo, C, and I C Dougall. "14/The Bible-1." Essay. In *What I
     Believe*, edited by J O Welsh, 36–37. Nairobi, Kenya: PCEA
     Jitegemea Publishers, 2009.

38 Ibid

39 Ibid

40 Ibid

41 Ibid

---

[42] This is the translation of the Apostles Creed that was issued by the Pope's Congregation for Divine Worship and Discipline of the Sacrament in June 2008 a copy of which was retrieved from Tierney, James. "The Apostles' Creed." Cardinal Newman Faith Resources Inc, October 7, 2008. https://www.cardinalnewman.com.au/downloads.

[43] Kiongo, C, and I C Dougall. "14/The Bible-1." Essay. In *What I Believe*, edited by J O Welsh, 36–37. Nairobi, Kenya: PCEA Jitegemea Publishers, 2009.

[44] Pecorino, Philip A. *Online Textbook*. Accessed March 30, 2020. https://www.qcc.cuny.edu/SocialSciences/ppecorino/PHIL_of_RELIGION_TEXT/TABLE_of_CONTENTS.htm.

[45] Ibid

[46] Timmons, Greg. "Muhammad." Biography.com. A&E Networks Television, November 5, 2019. https://www.biography.com/religious-figure/muhammad.

[47] Ibid

[48] "Religions - Islam: The Qur'an." BBC. BBC, July 14, 2011. https://www.bbc.co.uk/religion/religions/islam/texts/Qur'an_1.shtml.

[49] Timmons, Greg. "Muhammad." Biography.com. A&E Networks Television, November 5, 2019. https://www.biography.com/religious-figure/muhammad.

[50] Ibid

[51] Ibid

[52] Ibid

[53] Ibid

[54] Pecorino, Philip A. *Online Textbook*. Accessed March 30, 2020. https://www.qcc.cuny.edu/SocialSciences/ppecorino/PHIL_of_RELIGION_TEXT/TABLE_of_CONTENTS.htm.

[55] Warraq, Ibn. *Why I Am Not a Muslim*. Amherst, NY: Prometheus Books, 2003.

[56] Ibid

[57] Ibid

[58] *Holy Books: The Qur'an*. YouTube video, 10.04, A film by Kim Roden, April 20, 2018.

https://www.youtube.com/watch?v=ABkhC-QHG34&t=327s.

59 Ibid

60 Warraq, Ibn. *Why I Am Not a Muslim*. Amherst, NY: Prometheus Books, 2003.

61 Ibid

62 *Holy Books: The Qur'an*. YouTube video, 10.04, A film by Kim Roden, April 20, 2018. https://www.youtube.com/watch?v=ABkhC-QHG34&t=327s.

63 Pecorino, Philip A. *Online Textbook*. Accessed March 30, 2020. https://www.qcc.cuny.edu/SocialSciences/ppecorino/PHIL_of_RELIGION_TEXT/TABLE_of_CONTENTS.htm.

64 "Hadith and the Corruption of the Great Religion of Islam: Submission.org - Your Best Source for Submission (Islam)." Hadith and the Corruption of the great religion of Islam | Submission.org - Your best source for Submission (Islam). Accessed April 2, 2020. https://submission.org/Corruption_of_Religion.html.

65 Ibid

66 Ibid.

67 Islam, J.A. (2020). The Difference Between Hadith and Sunna. Retrieved on 2 April, 2020 from http://quransmessage.com/articles/hadith%20and%20sunna%20FM3.htm.

68 "Religions - Islam: Basic Articles of Faith." BBC. BBC, July 19, 2011. https://www.bbc.co.uk/religion/religions/islam/beliefs/beliefs.shtml.

69 "Al-Qur'an Al-Kareem - القرآن الكريم." Surah Al-Kafirun [109:6]. Accessed April 2, 2020. https://quran.com/109/6.

70 "Hinduism." Sacred. Accessed April 3, 2020. https://www.sacred-texts.com/hin/index.htm.

71 Ibid

72 Ibid

73 Ibid

74 Ibid

---

75 Ibid

76 Basu, Anindita. "Mahabharata." Ancient History
     Encyclopedia. Ancient History Encyclopedia, April 20,
     2020. https://www.ancient.eu/Mahabharata/.

77 "Hinduism." Sacred. Accessed April 3, 2020.
     https://www.sacred-texts.com/hin/index.htm.

78 Ibid

79 Ibid

80 *What Is Hinduism. What Is Hinduism?* Cogito, 2019.
     https://www.youtube.com/watch?v=xlBEEuYIWwY.

81 The Editors of Encyclopaedia Britannica. "Pali Canon."
     Encyclopædia Britannica. Encyclopædia Britannica, inc.,
     March 22, 2019.
     https://www.britannica.com/topic/Tipitaka.

82 "Pāli Canon." Wikiwand. Accessed April 11, 2020.
     https://www.wikiwand.com/en/P%C4%81li_Canon.

83 Ibid

84 "Early Buddhism: Three Baskets of Dharma." *Dharma*, 2017,
     34–59. https://doi.org/10.1515/9780824860639-006.

85 Buddhism. Accessed April 22, 2020.
     https://www.qcc.cuny.edu/SocialSciences/ppecorino/PHI
     L_of_RELIGION_TEXT/CHAPTER_2_RELIGIONS/Buddh
     ism.htm.

86 Ibid

87 Ibid

88 Ibid

89 Ibid

90 Ibid

91 Ibid

92 Ibid

93 Ibid

94 Ibid

95 Beyers, Jaco. "Religion and Culture: Revisiting a Close
     Relative." *HTS Teologiese Studies / Theological Studies* 73,
     no. 1 (2017). https://doi.org/10.4102/hts.v73i1.3864.

96 Urdang, Laurence. *The Oxford Desk Dictionary*. New York:
     Oxford University Press, 1995.

97 "Who Are the Taliban?" BBC News. BBC, February 27, 2020.
https://www.bbc.com/news/world-south-asia-11451718.

98 Ibid

99 Ibid

100 Roy, Arundhati. "The Disconnect between Religion and Culture." Eurozine, August 20, 2015.
https://www.eurozine.com/the-disconnect-between-religion-and-culture/.

101 Ibid

102 Bezhan, Frud. "Afghans Lift Lid On Sports Under The Taliban." RadioFreeEurope/RadioLiberty. Radio Free Europe / Radio Liberty, July 11, 2012.
https://www.rferl.org/a/afghans-recall-sports-under-the-taliban/24642278.html.

103 Rathje, W. "Why the Taliban Are Destroying Buddhas." USA Today. Gannett Satellite Information Network. Accessed April 26, 2020.
https://usatoday30.usatoday.com/news/science/archaeology/2001-03-22-afghan-buddhas.htm.

104 "Afghan Conflict: US and Taliban Sign Deal to End 18-Year War." BBC News. BBC, February 29, 2020.
https://www.bbc.com/news/world-asia-51689443.

105 Ibid

106 Ibid

107 Okeke, Chukwuma O., Christopher N. Ibenwa, and Gloria Tochukwu Okeke. "Conflicts Between African Traditional Religion and Christianity in Eastern Nigeria: The Igbo Example." *SAGE Open* 7, no. 2 (2017): 215824401770932.
https://doi.org/10.1177/2158244017709322.

108 Okeke, Henry Chukwudi. *Spirituality of the Igbo People of Nigeria an Example of Religious Modernization in a Global World.* S.l.: LIT VERLAG, 2020.

109 Ibid

110 Ibid

111 Okeke, Chukwuma O., Christopher N. Ibenwa, and Gloria Tochukwu Okeke. "Conflicts Between African Traditional Religion and Christianity in Eastern Nigeria: The Igbo

Example." *SAGE Open* 7, no. 2 (2017): 215824401770932.
    https://doi.org/10.1177/2158244017709322.

[112] Ibid

[113] Ibid

[114] Ibid

[115] Ibid

[116] Ibid

[117] Ibid

[118] Kenyatta, Jomo, and B. Malinowski. *Facing Mount Kenya*. New
    York: AMS Press, 1978

[119] Ibid

[120] Ibid

[121] Shell-Duncan, Bettina, David Gathara, and Zhuzhi Moore.
    "Female Genital Mutilation/Cutting in Kenya: Is Change
    Taking Place? Descriptive Statistics from Four Waves of
    Demographic and Health Surveys," 2017.
    https://doi.org/10.31899/rh7.1022.

[122] Kenyatta, Jomo, and B. Malinowski. *Facing Mount Kenya*. New
    York: AMS Press, 1978.

[123] Ibid

[124] Ibid

[125] Ibid

[126] Gathogo, Julius. "The Continuity of Indigenous Rituals in
    African Ecclesiology: A Kenyan Experience from a
    Historical Perspective." *STJ | Stellenbosch Theological
    Journal* 3, no. 1 (2017).
    https://doi.org/10.17570/stj.2017.v3n1.a06.

[127] Ibid

[128] "Chronology History." www.pcea.or.ke. Accessed April 15,
    2020. http://www.pcea.or.ke/index.php/helix-
    framework-6.

[129] User, Super. "Chronology History." www.pcea.or.ke, January
    1, 1891. http://www.pcea.or.ke/index.php/major-history.

[130] User, Super. "Chronology History." www.pcea.or.ke.
    Accessed April 14, 2020.
    http://www.pcea.or.ke/indexphp/helix-framework-6.

[131] Ibid

132 "COFFEE DEVELOPMENT AND MARKETING STRATEGY 2024-2029," 2024. https://kilimo.go.ke/wp-content/uploads/2024/03/Final-Draft-Coffee-Developemnt-and-Marketing-Strategy-27-Jan-2024-1.pdf.

133 Presbyterian Church of East Africa - World Council of Churches, September 25, 2013. https://www.oikoumene.org/en/member-churches/presbyterian-church-of-east-africa.

134 Shell-Duncan, Bettina, David Gathara, and Zhuzhi Moore. "Female Genital Mutilation/Cutting in Kenya: Is Change Taking Place? Descriptive Statistics from Four Waves of Demographic and Health Surveys," 2017. https://doi.org/10.31899/rh7.1022.

135 Kenyatta, Jomo, and B. Malinowski. *Facing Mount Kenya*. New York: AMS Press, 1978.

136 Ibid

137 Ibid

138 "PCEA Church's Attack on Gikuyu Culture Is Wrong." kenya2uhub, May 29, 2018. https://www.kenya2uhub.com/plots-houses-property-apartments/pcea-churchs-attack-on-gikuyu-culture-is-wrong/.

139 Komu, Nicholas. "PCEA Ban on Kikuyu Rite Sparks Storm." PCEA ban on Kikuyu rite sparks big storm. Daily Nation, May 24, 2018. https://mobile.nation.co.ke/news/PCEA-ban-on-Kikuyu-rite-sparks-big-storm/1950946-4577196-3rttsfz/index.html.

140 Ngugi, Muiru. "Modern Christian Life and Kikuyu Rituals." Medium. Medium, December 22, 2019. https://medium.com/@muirucngugi/modern-christian-life-and-kikuyu-rituals-433656d95f5d.

141 Komu, Nicholas. "PCEA Ban on Kikuyu Rite Sparks Storm." PCEA ban on Kikuyu rite sparks big storm. Daily Nation, May 24, 2018. https://mobile.nation.co.ke/news/PCEA-ban-on-Kikuyu-rite-sparks-big-storm/1950946-4577196-3rttsfz/index.html.

142 Ngwiri, Magesha. "NGWIRI: Church Should Clean House First before Chasing Harmless." Daily Nation. Daily Nation, June 1, 2018. https://www.nation.co.ke/oped/opinion/Church-should-clean-house-first/440808-4590866-hm2ghwz/index.html.

143 Gathogo, Julius. "The Continuity of Indigenous Rituals in African Ecclesiology: A Kenyan Experience from a Historical Perspective." *STJ | Stellenbosch Theological Journal* 3, no. 1 (2017). https://doi.org/10.17570/stj.2017.v3n1.a06.

144 Ibid

145 Seife, C. (2000). Vatican regrets burning cosmologist. Science Now. Archived from the original on 8 June 2013. Retrieved 28 June 2019.

146 Weksler, Benny. 2016. "Judge a Man by His Questions Rather than His Answers." *The Journal of Thoracic and Cardiovascular Surgery* 151 (1): 58–59. https://doi.org/10.1016/j.jtcvs.2015.08.089.

147 Brooks, Alison Wood, and Leslie K. John. "How to Ask Great Questions." Harvard Business Review, November 19, 2019. https://hbr.org/2018/05/the-surprising-power-of-questions.

148 Fitzgerald, Timothy. *Discourse on Civility and Barbarity*. New York: Oxford University Press, 2012.

149 Seife, C. (2000). Vatican regrets burning cosmologist. *Science Now. Archived from the original on 8 June 2013. Retrieved 28 June 2019.*

150 Mill, John Stuart. *Utilitarianism ; Liberty*. London: Dent, 1972.

151 "Donald Morgan." The Secular Web. Accessed April 7, 2020. https://infidels.org/library/modern/donald_morgan/.

152 El-Neil, Ibn. *The Truth About Islam*. New York, NY: Eloquent Books, 2008.

153 Warraq, Ibn. *Why I Am Not a Muslim*. Amherst, NY: Prometheus Books, 2003.

154 Ibid

155 Ibid

---

156 *The Cambridge History of Islam.* Cambridge: Cambridge Univ. Press, 1980.

157 Warraq, Ibn. *Why I Am Not a Muslim.* Amherst, NY: Prometheus Books, 2003.

158 Ibid

159 "Abrogation In The Koran - Muhammadanism." Accessed April 9, 2020. http://www.muhammadanism.org/Quran/abrogation_ko ran.pdf.

160 Dashti, Ali. *Twenty Three Years: a Study of the Prophetic Career of Mohammed.* People International, 1990.

161 "Hadith and the Corruption of the Great Religion of Islam: Submission.org - Your Best Source for Submission (Islam)." Hadith and the Corruption of the great religion of Islam | Submission.org - Your best source for Submission (Islam). Accessed April 2, 2020. https://submission.org/Corruption_of_Religion.html.

162 Ibid

163 Brown, Daniel. *Rethinking Tradition in Modern Islamic Thought.* New York: Cambridge, 1998.

164 "Contradictions in the Hadith." WikiIslam. Accessed April 10, 2020. https://wikiislam.net/wiki/Contradictions_in_the_Hadit h.

165 "QuranX.com The Most Complete Quran / Hadith / Tafsir Collection Available!" Sahih Bukhari Hadiths. Accessed April 10, 2020. https://quranx.com/hadith/Bukhari/In-Book/Book-67/Hadith-127/.

166 "QuranX.com The Most Complete Quran / Hadith / Tafsir Collection Available!" Sahih Bukhari Hadiths. Accessed April 10, 2020. https://quranx.com/hadith/Bukhari/In-Book/Book-77/Hadith-165/.

167 "QuranX.com The Most Complete Quran / Hadith / Tafsir Collection Available!" Sahih Bukhari Hadiths. Accessed April 10, 2020. https://quranx.com/hadith/Bukhari/In-Book/Book-59/Hadith-83/.

168 "QuranX.com The Most Complete Quran / Hadith / Tafsir Collection Available!" Sahih Bukhari Hadiths. Accessed

April 10, 2020. https://quranx.com/hadith/Bukhari/In-Book/Book-67/Hadith-6/.

169 "QuranX.com The Most Complete Quran / Hadith / Tafsir Collection Available!" Sahih Bukhari Hadiths. Accessed April 10, 2020. https://quranx.com/hadith/Bukhari/In-Book/Book-5/Hadith-21/.

170 "QuranX.com The Most Complete Quran / Hadith / Tafsir Collection Available!" Sahih Bukhari Hadiths. Accessed April 10, 2020. https://quranx.com/hadith/Bukhari/In-Book/Book-59/Hadith-74/.

171 "QuranX.com The Most Complete Quran / Hadith / Tafsir Collection Available!" Sahih Bukhari Hadiths. Accessed April 10, 2020. https://quranx.com/hadith/Bukhari/In-Book/Book-67/Hadith-31/.

172 "Why I Am Not a Hindu." The Secular Web. Accessed April 10, 2020. https://infidels.org/library/modern/ramendra_nath/hindu.html.

173 Violatti, Cristian. "The Vedas." Ancient History Encyclopedia. Ancient History Encyclopedia, April 8, 2020. https://www.ancient.eu/The_Vedas/.

174 "Why I Am Not a Hindu." The Secular Web. Accessed April 10, 2020. https://infidels.org/library/modern/ramendra_nath/hindu.html.

175 Violatti, Cristian. "The Vedas." Ancient History Encyclopedia. Ancient History Encyclopedia, April 8, 2020. https://www.ancient.eu/The_Vedas/.

176 "Why I Am Not a Hindu." The Secular Web. Accessed April 10, 2020. https://infidels.org/library/modern/ramendra_nath/hindu.html.

177 Ibid

178 Ibid.

179 Ibid.

180 Ibid

181 "The Gita's Setting Reflects Not Logical Absurdity but Metaphysical Urgency." Begin each day enriched with

181 nuggets of timeless wisdom Article By Chaitanya Charan Das. Accessed April 11, 2020. https://www.gitadaily.com/the-gitas-setting-reflects-not-logical-absurdity-but-metaphysical-urgency/.

182 Shankar, Ravi. "Contradictions in the Gita Helps One to Think - Times of India." The Times of India. The Times of India, December 23, 2009. https://timesofindia.indiatimes.com/Contradictions-in-the-Gita-helps-one-to-think/articleshow/4910701.cms.

183 "The Teaching of the Bhagavad Gita." Comparative Religion - Possible difficulties in the philosophy of the Bhagavad Gita. Accessed April 10, 2020. https://www.comparativereligion.com/Gita.html.

184 Ibid.

185 Soka Gakkai International. "The Enlightenment of Women." Soka Gakkai International (SGI), July 17, 2008. https://www.sgi.org/about-us/buddhist-concepts/the-enlightenment-of-women.html.

186 Abeysekara, Ananda. "The Saffron Army, Violence, Terror(ism): Buddhism, Identity, and Difference in Sri Lanka." *Numen* 48, no. 1 (2001): 1-46. Accessed April 11, 2020. www.jstor.org/stable/3270564.

187 Jerryson, Michael K., and Mark Juergensmeyer. *Buddhist Warfare*. Oxford: Oxford University Press, 2010.

188 Pecorino, Philip A. *Online Textbook*. Accessed March 30, 2020. https://www.qcc.cuny.edu/SocialSciences/ppecorino/PHIL_of_RELIGION_TEXT/default.htm

189 Ibid

190 Del Soldato, Eva. "Natural Philosophy in the Renaissance." Stanford Encyclopedia of Philosophy. Stanford University, April 8, 2019. https://plato.stanford.edu/entries/natphil-ren/.

191 Meister, Chad. "Philosophy of Religion." Internet Encyclopedia of Philosophy. Accessed April 5, 2020. https://www.iep.utm.edu/religion/.

192 Ibid.

193 Meister, Chad. "Philosophy of Religion." Internet Encyclopedia of Philosophy. Accessed April 5, 2020. https://www.iep.utm.edu/religion/.

194 Admin. "Philosophy Jokes." Puns and One Liners, November 20, 2015. https://punsandoneliners.com/randomness/philosophy-jokes/.

195 "Heidegger, Martin – Being and Time [Trans. Macquarrie …" Accessed April 13, 2020. https://docs.google.com/file/d/0BylvcBG7_xG_bzVkQUxS bnk1ODg/edit.

196 Meister, Chad. "Philosophy of Religion." Internet Encyclopedia of Philosophy. Accessed April 5, 2020. https://www.iep.utm.edu/religion/.

197 Ibid

198 Ibid

199 Hick, John. *Philosophy of Religion*. Englewood Cliffs, NJ: Prentice Hall, 1990.

200 Runzo, Joseph. "God, Commitment, and Other Faiths: Pluralism vs Relativism." *World Views and Perceiving God*, 1993, 193–218. https://doi.org/10.1007/978-1-349-23106-5_9.

201 Meister, Chad. *Introducing Philosophy of Religion*. London: Routledge, 2009.

202 Ibid

203 Ibid

204 Craig, William Lane., and Quentin Smith. *Theism, Atheism, and Big Bang Cosmology*. Oxford: Clarendon Press, 1993.

205 Reichenbach, Bruce. "Cosmological Argument." Stanford Encyclopedia of Philosophy. Stanford University, October 11, 2017. https://plato.stanford.edu/entries/cosmological-argument/.

206 Meister, Chad. "Philosophy of Religion." Internet Encyclopedia of Philosophy. Accessed April 5, 2020. https://www.iep.utm.edu/religion/.

207 Ibid

208 Ibid

209 Ibid

---

210 Ibid

211 Ibid

212 "A History of the Bible: Who Wrote It and When?"
HistoryExtra, April 8, 2020.
https://www.historyextra.com/period/ancient-
history/history-bible-origins-who-wrote-when-how-
reliable-historical-record/.

213 Teja, Sai, University of Hyderabad, and University of
Hyderabad. "#1 Most Beautiful Equation in Mathematics
– Euler's Identity." ScienceHook, May 29, 2019.
https://sciencehook.com/equations/eulers-identity-1682.

214 Lexico Dictionary. Retrieved from
https://www.lexico.com/en/definition/faith

215 *Faith: The Story of Abraham*, YouTube video, 8.51, "Stephen
Hicks", February 8, 2010.
https://www.youtube.com/watch?v=4iEAOtZMS3Q&list=P
L5CB5A1E2D9F4E6A2&index=24.

216 Billy Graham Evangelic Association (2015). 9 Ways to Grow
in Your Faith. Retrieved on 28 June, 2019 from
https://billygraham.org/story/9-ways-to-grow-in-
your-faith/

217 Jordan, R.B. (2012). Three Ways to Increase Your Faith.
Retrieved on 28 June, 2019 from
https://www.crosswalk.com/faith/spiritual-life/three-
ways-to-increase-your-faith.html

218 "The Official Rules of Golf," R&A, n.d.,
https://www.randa.org/rog/the-rules-of-golf.

Books by This Author

Shamba Shenanigans: A Collection Of Riveting True Stories

A collection of riveting true-life experiences. Some stories are hilarious; others are thought-provoking, and others are likely to evoke different emotions as the story unfolds. Each story has one or more helpful life lessons.

The Endless Search for More: A Collection Of True Stories On Money Matters

A collection of true stories that revolve around our continuous search for "more." And while this trait is essential for the long-term sustainability of humanity, John Mucai suggests that we must always strive to appropriately calibrate our desires. And more importantly, adopt a problem-solving mindset in our never-ending quest for "more."

John Mucai

Ngurario: A Traditional Kikuyu Marriage Experience

Ngurario is a true story of the multiple steps that John and Susan went through to formalize their marriage according to Kikuyu traditions. The book delves deeply into the drama, excitement, and joy they experienced along the way, right up to the final step in the journey, namely, an elaborate and colorful ceremony called *ngurario*.

Historical Snapshots of The Great: What Can We Learn from Them?

The quality of life we enjoy today is a function of the many commendable actions taken by individuals in different spheres of life. Some of these people came before us many years ago, while others live among us. This book explores the lives of some significant historical figures to determine whether they share any common attributes we can emulate.

Multiple Dilemmas: A Fictional Story of Multiple Ethical Dilemmas Based on True Historical Events

Multiple Dilemmas is a thriller based on historical events that raise significant ethical questions. The book delves deeply into challenging situations where ethical considerations are paramount, but the right choices are unclear. The twists and turns in the story will keep the reader entranced for several hours.

Reminiscing On Basics: Fascinating Science and Maths Ideas for Everyone

Some ideas in science and math are so fascinating that it is a shame they are inaccessible to many people. This book attempts to fill the gap. Perhaps the curiosity triggered by these ideas will set a new intellectual journey into motion for some people, as it has done for the author.

One Day in The Year 3000

Nobody knows what the future holds one thousand years from now. But one can make some wild guesses. This book peeks into that distant future.

John Mucai

Archetypes Of Human Existence: A New Perspective

No two of the more than seven billion people inhabiting the earth are exactly the same. Even tweens have differences. Every individual has been bestowed unique attributes by nature. And yet, the behavior of human beings can be reduced to a few archetypes. At the heart of the matter, each human being is composed of a mind and a physical body, a mind that yearns for happiness and a body that longs for sustenance. And the interplay of these two needs creates the different archetypes of humans. This book explores a few of the archetypes. It discusses how the ideas around archetypes converge to offer a new perspective on fundamental questions that existentialists have grappled with for ages. The people described in the second chapter of this book are entirely fictitious. Any resemblance of their names to real people is purely coincidental. However, the characters are real and live among us. You may recognize some of them in your local community, your network of friends, or even in other human networks to which you are directly or indirectly connected.

Stratagem: Developing A Strategic Mindset

Have you ever attended a strategy meeting and wondered whether everyone in the forum understood what strategy meant? If you have, you are not alone. Interestingly, many such meetings roll on smoothly with impressive outcomes. That phenomenon is the ninth wonder of the world. Some participants probably spend many hours after the meeting engrossed in self-doubt or guilt, depending upon how loudly they spoke during the session. A cold or hot beverage usually works wonders during such moments of self-reflection. If you experience self-doubt but usually emerge from strategy discussions with your conscience intact, you must count your blessings. You are a brave survivor. But whatever category you belong to, you have the cure for strategy fuzziness right at your fingertips. Stratagem describes strategy with exceptional lucidity. Well-thought-out strategies are not only essential for business success; they are critical for success in personal life.

Number One: Nothing Else Seems to Count

In the modern, highly competitive world, doing well in any competition is not enough. Being number one is what counts. This book traces the lives of five colorful individuals. From the early stages of their lives, they have been winners in their unique ways.

We intimately experience the twists and turns that occur as they enter early adulthood and get embroiled in a contest anchored in pursuing business success and love. Each character will realize that things can become highly complex, emotionally draining, and even dangerous when love is in the mix. The outcome of their respective pursuits to be "number one" is astounding. Indeed, the way the story ends offers readers tremendous food for thought.

Fun and Grit: Encounters of Farming Hobbyists

The stories in this book are primarily about people—the people of the shamba (small farm). After working for one of the biggest multinational companies and dabbling in a small-scale farming hobby, I have come to the conclusion that every experience we have in life, whether pleasant or unpleasant, gives life its flavor.

Indeed, some unpleasant experiences add more spice to life. Having a nice laugh about something is often the magic trick. Laughter is undoubtedly the best medicine for the soul.

Index

John Mucai